Intimacy with God and my Well-worn Bible

Wesley J Allen

Published by Wesley J Allen, 2024.

While every precaution has been taken in the preparation of this book, the publisher assumes no responsibility for errors or omissions, or for damages resulting from the use of the information contained herein.

INTIMACY WITH GOD AND MY WELL-WORN BIBLE

First edition. April 6, 2024.

ISBN: 979-8224461158

Written by Wesley J Allen.

Table of Contents

Intimacy with God
and my well-worn Bible

Author: Wesley J Allen

Acknowledgements

Kind acknowledgement is made of all who helped me in carrying out this drama in my life. Some are mentioned in this book by initial only. Thus, they are not listed here by name for the desire to remain anonymous. They can recognize their place in the story. We give all the glory to God for He is the writer of the script. None of these things can happen in anyone's life unless God be the author. So, here are my wonderful helpers and friends by initial only:

JB: who baptized me into Christ 27 years ago and helped me to take the baby steps in my walk with Jesus.

AS: who has been a wonderful friend for nine years now, though our relationship is up and down because of my own hard-headedness. Without her I would never have started fasting and consequently would not have begun the Bible reading.

JP: who was appointed by God and led by the Spirit to give me encouragement when I most needed it. Without her I probably would have died.

DJ: who unknowingly gave the book its title because of her great dedication to God and desire for intimacy with Him.

RM: who was so excited about fasting with us. Miracles have happened in his life too that aren't written in this book.

RD: who thought my faith was so great during adversity. Her comments kept me hanging in there and helped give me strength for endurance and to build my faith.

BJ: who is my wonderful real estate friend. Without her I wouldn't live in this peaceful place. God directed her steps & made things happen for me to have this earthly home.

JR: who is my twin. Isn't that something? I was always Junior (Jr.) during childhood. Now she has carried that brand longer than I have.

RS: who was my wonderful employer. He always made sure I was well taken care of, considered me his best man, and in the end provided for my retirement.

And there is a host of others who I can't think of to mention who have helped to make my life wonderful. We each play a special part in someone's drama on Earth. We will all make a big wave in the mighty throng of Heaven.

Table of Contents

Introduction

I am what I am by the grace of God I am. There is no way that I even deserve to be a part of God's Kingdom. But ***blessed be God who has not turned away my prayer, nor His mercy from me***. Psalms 66:20

I am the "chiefest of sinners" as Apostle Paul said. I am the "vilest offender" as we sing in the song; and my eyes leak water when I sing that hymn. But I truly believe, and God has done wonders in my life. He uses the small, the foolish, and the baser to confound the wisdom of the wise. So, He uses me for special reasons.

I love to tell of His blessings; and He keeps blessing me all the more while I do. I go from person to person all across the nation telling the stories of the amazing things God has done in my life. They boggle my mind and that of others too.

In this book I will tell of my Bible reading experiences. I will tell you about fasting and prayer experiences. I will tell of my dedication to God of all that I am and all that I have; and how He has blessed me beyond all that I could dream or imagine because of it.

I don't tell you this to be bragging; but in the Lord I will boast. I tell of my blessings so that your faith may be increased. ***"...from faith, to faith... for the righteous man shall live by faith..."*** Romans 1:17 When we tell of our blessings to non-Christians, it warms their hearts and God can draw them to Himself. When we tell of our blessings to Christians it builds our faith. When we tell of them, God blesses even more.

I hope you will imitate the good things you see in me and turn away from anything evil. I know that your life will be blessed beyond measure if you will dedicate it to God. I hope for all the blessings you will read here to be yours, and many more besides.

I write this most especially in hopes that it will help someone. And I write it so that you can see what reading God's remarkable book, the Bible, can do for your life, for your character, and for the renewing of your mind.

I want to tell you of my Bible reading experiences so that you'll know that it is possible for you to do it too. I will tell you of all the benefits of reading the Bible. I will even tell you the time it takes to read the Bible from cover to cover. I will give you a generalization of how much time you will have to spend in God's book each day to read it completely through in forty days. I will tell you why that is much better than reading it in scattered bits for a whole year.

Many blessings
on your journey,

Wesley J. Allen

Published September 13, 2006

Chapter 1
Redeemed

First, I will give you my testimony, so you'll know where I came from and how I managed to get into God's Kingdom, a place I never dreamed of being. I had always known that I could never be good enough to go to Heaven or even be a part of God's people. Christianity was not for me. It wasn't that I didn't believe in God; but I just knew He would never accept me. But all that changed in a moment, in the blink of an eye.

Now, I really do cherish the love of my brothers and sisters; but you would not have so easily loved the Wes I used to be. All through my past I was guilty of all those "deeds of the flesh" listed in Galatians 5:19-21, all summed up under one word, <u>sin</u>. And all I knew about God was that He was there to punish me; and I just couldn't be good. I had tried many times to accept Jesus into my heart, like I was told, but it didn't work. I just couldn't stop doing all those bad things.

I describe myself back then as a "beer-drinking, cigarette-smoking, cussing, foul- mouthed, backwoods country boy who dressed like a countryside goat-roper." And I was no different at the time I got married except that I had gained an immediate sense of responsibility to my family. But still my greatest aspiration was to own my own go-cart track.

I was a very hard-worker and dedicated employee. My boss saw that I had potential and gave me a copy of "Acres of Diamonds." Through it I learned that I could do something better with my life. My wife and I joined the Amway business. I saw that Amway people were happy all the time. They had love and respect for each other. They were upbeat and positive.

They were going places with their lives. And they talked a lot. I wanted those things in my life. I hated people. I was sad and angry much of the time. I was inhibited and self-centered. I couldn't talk to one person let alone a group. Anger and hatred churning in my stomach caused me to be sick all the time.

I had been to see many doctors for this sickness. But no one could tell me what caused it or how to make it go away. Then one day when I was visiting a new doctor trying to find hope the doctor felt of my stomach and said, "I can tell you exactly what is wrong." Your stomach is churning ninety miles an hour. You have in turned aggression. You have got to start loving people and everything. He showed me the churning in my stomach with a sonogram. I knew exactly what I needed to do.

I discovered that most Amway people belonged to some Church. I decided I wanted to go to Church. But I didn't know anything about Church. My wife's aunt and uncle, who sponsored us into the Amway business, went to The Polytechnic Christian Church, so we went there for several Sundays.

One Sunday morning the preacher asked me, "Wes, don't you think it's about time?" I would not have known what he was talking about except that my wife and I had just been talking, and she told me that people get baptized in order to belong to a Church. So, I said, "Yes, I think it's about time." I responded to the invitation that day, and my wife followed. They didn't keep their baptistery full and had to make arrangements for us to be baptized the following Sunday.

The preacher came to visit us at home during the week. He asked if I had any questions. I was too ignorant to know what to ask, so I said, "No." After he left, my wife and I talked about it and decided we didn't know what we were doing. We decided not to go back there. We wanted to go to a different Church the following Sunday. I didn't know the location of any Church. I remembered having seen The Meadowbrook Methodist Church high on a hill. I didn't know exactly where, but I put on my best goat-roper boots, and we headed in that direction. In only a short distance I saw a Church. I said, "Look! There's a Church, and the parking lot is full, and people are going in. Let's stop here!" And so, we did. And we stayed ten years.

Right after the service that day JB, the outreach minister, invited himself to our house to study the Bible with us. When he arrived, he said, "Wes, I need to ask you some questions to find out what you know so I'll know where to begin the study." I said, "Why don't we start at the beginning? I don't know anything!" I didn't even know where the beginning was. He started in John, not Genesis.

Several weeks later I responded to the invitation, knowing very little more than my sins were going to be forgiven. And my wife followed. We were both baptized that day by immersion in water for the forgiveness of our sins. And you know something? It worked this time! From that day on God began molding and making me into the Wes I am today. It wasn't all easy going. And even after giving my heart to God there are some things I've done that I regret. But I never took my heart back, so God changed even that, and made all those things work together for good.

Today I am satisfied with my life. I really love all the talents and abilities God gave me; and I use them to bless His people. I love people and I go about doing "good" like Jesus did. And you know that churning in my stomach? Gone! I lost it before it developed into an ulcer. The thing God taught me that changed my life more than anything else is: My only purpose here is to give and receive love and forgiveness. When I practice that, I'm walking in the steps of Jesus.

Chapter 2
Life Dealt me an Ace

Early Christianity was a thrill much of the time; but it was tough going too. It was an uphill climb. Every time I did something good, God was right there with His blessings. When I did something bad, He was very patient with me. My life was moving up fast.

It was on October 28th of 1979 that my wife and I gave our hearts to God. About two weeks later we were invited to attend a Positive Thinking Rally at the Fort Worth Convention Center along with the outreach minister and his wife. Let's just call them Mr. and Mrs. JB.

Positive Thinking was right up my alley, for my wife and I had recently joined the Amway Business, and I was learning that I could do something with my life. I didn't have to remain the backwoods country boy I had grown up to be. It was possible for me to change and become somebody.

Up to this point in my life, age 24, I was like Country Bumpkin come to town. My greatest aspiration had been to own my own go-kart track. Mr. JB had taught me how to tie a necktie and wear dress clothes to church instead of my ragged roper jeans. So we attended this Positive Thinking Rally.

We listened to Motivational Speakers like Zig Ziglar, Dennis Waitley, Norman Vincent Peale, and others. Then it was Billy Burden's turn to speak. He was the Memory Master. Coming into the Convention Center he had met 100 people, locked their names into memory, and gave them his business card.

As he walked up onto the stage, he had everyone stand to whom he had given a business card and a reserved seat near the front. Then he proceeded to give them back their names without missing even one.

Mr. JB was so impressed with that, and with all the Memory Techniques Billy Burden had talked about. He wanted to get one of the Memory Courses and begin learning immediately so he could remember the names of everyone who came into the church.

I was still a bit too ignorant to be impressed. Maybe the go-kart track still held more attraction to me. I probably knew about a dozen people, and I didn't have any trouble remembering their names.

The Memory Course cost $120.00 and Mr. JB wanted one. But he didn't want to spend that much, so he asked me if I'd go halves with him. I had not yet developed the ability to say "No" so I said, "Okay."

Mr. JB took the Memory Course home, copied the tapes and all the printed material, kept the copies for himself and gave me the originals. That's what Christians do. Give away the best and keep the lesser for themselves. I was learning.

Now, when I pay $60.00 for something, I'm at least going to examine it to see what I bought. I listened to the first cassette tape, and I was immediately fascinated. In about 30 minutes I had learned the first 50 mental hooks and I was locking things into memory right and left.

In a short time I could do everything with the Memory Techniques that Billy Burden could do. And I adapted them to suit my own needs. I had already moved on past Country Bumpkin, got a GED Diploma, and was attending college.

I "aced" everything in college and graduated with high honors because I had Memory Techniques. Professors would excuse me from taking tests and final exams at times saying, "You'll just get another "A," and an "F" wouldn't hurt your grade point average.

Four years after that Positive Thinking Rally, I wrote to Billy Burden and told him what I had been doing with his Memory Techniques and how I had adapted them to suit my needs. He invited my wife and me to come to Clearwater, Florida and attend a Memory Training Seminar. It cost $500.00 per person to attend; but for us it was free.

At that seminar I helped Billy Burden do memory demonstrations, and I gave a little talk on Student Memory. And I became a distributor for the Billy Burden Memory Master Method cassette tape course.

In a short time, I developed my own strategy for teaching people the Memory Techniques. Now I'm 51 years old, and I have used and taught Memory Techniques for 27 years. I have given them away in some cases, I have sold many Memory Courses, and I have developed my own specialty, memorizing long documents of History and Scripture. I memorize at the rate of 1000 words per hour.

Memory Techniques aren't for everyone. My wife never learned the techniques, and Mr. JB never did anything with his Memory Course. I didn't teach my kids the techniques; but I showed my two daughters some strategies for remembering that kept them "A" students all the way through school.

God was preparing me all along for what He had in mind for my future. It wasn't my idea to memorize scripture or history. God led me to that. He assigned all my memory projects. I had learned to discern His every prompting. With this story I'm way past the end of my marriage. Memory Techniques began very early in my walk with God, and they haven't ended yet. Let me back up now to tell of God's molding and making me into the Wes that I am today.

Chapter 3
Mold me and make me after Thy Will

For the first five years of Christianity, I studied the Bible intensely. I did correspondence courses, I graded correspondence courses, I wrote letters of encouragement, I even taught the Junior High Sunday School Class. And I took a mission trip to Mexico with two other guys. While we were there we achieved the smile of God. God walked with me down streets of uncertainty. He molded me in every way to bring out the best. Committed, I followed.

There came a time when I decided to build the kids a go kart. Actually, it was mostly for me. The dream of owning your own go kart track doesn't go away easily. I built the frame, welded it together, and found or made all the parts I needed for wheels, brakes, and steering. Then I got out an engine, and was cleaning it off, shining it up, and making it ready for a nice clean little kart. As I was scraping off grease, I noticed a company name and address stamped into the crankcase. It said, "Strawn Rentals."

Oh, oh, now I remember where this engine came from. Before I became a Christian, I was a two-bit thief at times. One time my brother and I had been bar hopping, and we pulled up in front of Embers Lounge, and parked beside a truck with an intriguing apparatus in the back. I didn't even know what it was; but I said to my brother, "I believe that thing would look better in the back of my truck. So, we hoisted it over the sides of both trucks and left immediately to take it home. Later that night my brother and I ended up in the drunk tank. I talked to God about getting us out of there without getting in trouble for theft and promised never to drink any alcoholic beverages again. That was one of those times that I called on God when I was in trouble. Before I knew Him, I knew that He could help me and might if I promised to be good. He got us out, I kept my promise, and soon after that I became a Christian. He had saved my life several times before I even knew Him. He gave me grace and mercy before I ever gave my heart to Him.

I think that apparatus was an exterminating pump for treating under a cement slab for termites. I dismantled it the next day, salvaged the engine and other parts, and stored them away for future use. Now when I remembered where I had acquired that engine, being a Christian now, I was immediately pierced in my heart. And God prompted me to put it back together and take it back to Strawn Rentals and confess what I had done. And He further prompted me to take back everything I had in my possession that was stolen and confess to each person that I had stolen something from him or her.

I took tools back to companies I had worked for. I paid a guy $8.00 I had beaten him out of. I put myself at plenty of risk of being arrested. But God had said, "Do it!" And I obeyed and trusted Him for the final outcome. I didn't beat around the bush or cut myself any slack. I told each person outright, "I stole these things from you. I don't have any excuses. I just saw them, wanted them, and took them. I justified it by thinking that you had much and I had little."

I have long since learned that God, working through our lives, can reach the hearts of people without us even knowing a thing about it. One of my former employers, to whom I had returned tools, tried several times to hire me back. Each time my current employer would give me a raise to stay with him. On one of those occasions the former employer said to me, "Wes, you have had a greater influence on my life than any man I know." Whether he was talking about the returning of the tools or not, I don't know. But maybe God reached his heart through that. And what influence it had on the others, I don't know. God is in control!

Chapter 4
Instantaneous Healing

God has taught me many things through various incidents in my life. He literally snatched me out of the arms of death several times. My five kids never knew anything but the Christian life. My wife and I and the kids would do good things for people around the neighborhood. We loved to visit nursing homes and extend love to the elderly who couldn't get out and do anything. We would take gifts for them on Easter and Christmas. We would sing for them. We would read scripture.

Early in my walk with God, He gave me an instantaneous healing experience. My dad broke my back when I was ten years old. He was punishing me for something, and he picked me up above his head and slammed me down on his bed. Then he smashed his fist into the middle of my back. Then he said, "Now get out of here." Gladly I would, but I could barely move, my lower back and hips hurt so much. I managed to get out of there without letting him see that I was hurt.

There was no telling anyone about it. I certainly couldn't talk to my mom or any other grownups. And it was unheard of to go to a doctor. I suffered the pain for a few days, and then it went away. It would come back from time to time, and I would suffer for a few days, hardly able to walk or climb steps in school. Other students would laugh at me. But I could never tell them what was wrong. It had to be kept a secret.

Those episodes of pain came back from time to time on into adulthood. Once when I was at work at age 18 the pain came on the job. Immediately, my supervisor sent me to the doctor. Even then I couldn't and didn't tell anyone where I first experienced that injury. The doctor x-rayed my back and told me that a part of my spinal column was out of place. He said a chunk of bone was missing from the 2nd Lumbar Vertebrae, and on the 5th Lumbar Vertebrae the Transverse process was too long on one side, touching the Pelvic Girdle, and broken off on the other side. Below is a picture of the skeleton so you can picture these bones. (That old boy does look like me, a little green around the gills.)

When looking at the picture below, if you hold down the control key on your keyboard and move the roll switch on your mouse, you can increase or decrease the size of the picture and the text.

On his right the Pelvic Girdle is pointed out.

The 5th Lumbar Vertebrae is between the tops of them, in green, on top of the Sacrum.

The little stubs of bone protruding from each side are Transverse Processes. One was touching the Pelvic and the other was broken off.

The 2nd Lumbar Vertebrae, 3 discs up, was out of place

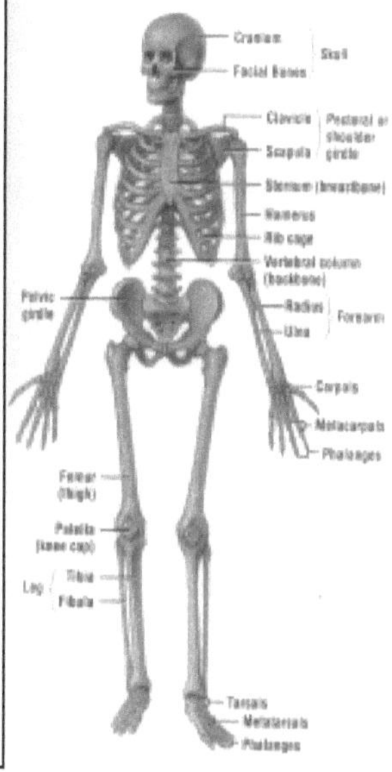

The pain came back from time to time between the ages of ten and twenty-five. It came back for the last time at age twenty-five. My family and I were in church on a Sunday morning. When we stood up to sing, the pain suddenly came and I could hardly stand up. As we sang, the pain left, and it never came back. I wish I could remember the title of that powerful song! After age thirty I have suffered back pain from other causes, namely the stresses of life. My back has been x-rayed many times. No doctor has ever told me about those bone structural problems again. They're gone!

Chapter 5
The Building of a Carpenter

I started working for RS Mfg. at age twenty-four, in the prime of my youth, building furniture. I gave it my "everything." I always tried to work as if I were working for the Lord. He blessed me tremendously. He trained me and caused me to grow in favor with my employer. I considered myself a carpenter, like Jesus, and became one of the very best. My skill grew in building furniture, but it didn't stop there, for I gave my heart totally to God in the first month of my employment. I have built everything from little boxes to a model of our solar system with all nine planets orbiting and rotating around the sun. I have built buildings, remodeled some, refinished antiques, and some of my furniture is even in the Kimball Art Museum.

When I started working at RS Mfg. I didn't even know how to read a blueprint. I worked for Toppy's Millwork for three years but always worked off a shop drawing. RS would be going over a job with me, something he wanted me to build, pointing out the way he expected everything to be done. I would be listening intently. My mind was busy putting the symbols I recognized together with what I didn't know, and trying to make sense of it all, while listening to what the boss was saying. RS would often say, "Wes, I don't know if you're getting this, you're not saying anything." I would say, "RS, I'll handle it!"

When I got busy gathering material for the job, I would often stare at the print dumbfounded, still not knowing what all those lines and symbols meant. I would pray, "Lord, please open my eyes and let me see what I'm looking at." He did it every time! Within minutes it would be clear to me what I was to build. Thus, I grew with God's help! Every time I turned around RS gave me a raise, or a bonus. My ex-employer kept trying to hire me back, but he could never match RS's offer to me. It was sometimes after making a big costly mistake that I would get a raise. I asked my supervisor about it once. I had always tried to give some suggestions for fixing it. He said, "Wes, the man who isn't making any mistakes isn't doing anything."

Chapter 6

Here Comes the Wrecking Ball

I was thrilled with the change that had come about in me. It was not by my own effort. Sin held no attraction to me (well mostly). I was walking on a higher plane except for my one overwhelming evil vice that had plagued my life from my youth up. I couldn't keep complete control of the deepest, darkest part of my sinful nature.

In due time my marriage broke up and my life bottomed out. I was put outside the door like Fred Flintstone's cat, except, without the milk bottle. Now I had to learn to walk through life alone. I had to climb all the mountains by myself; and they loomed high in front of me. I held onto the God of Heaven and prayed a lot, out loud, because I have an easily distracted psyche. If I pray silently my mind wanders. At the age of thirty-three it was still too young to be out alone. I was on an intense life-change program.

So, the castle of my life was knocked down to the very foundation. But it was anchored to the Rock. I lost everything for which I had worked hard for over fifteen years. But one thing that couldn't be taken from me was my relationship with God and all that He was building into my heart. I was never to return to the old life. The precious little wife of my youth did return there; and pulled the kids along with her. Now, glory to His name, these seventeen years later she regrets it. But I love my life. It's just God and me. We've been everywhere, and we do everything together.

Chapter 7
Pulled Up by my Bootstraps

Out of the mud and the miry clay He lifted me and set my feet on solid ground. The next several years brought lots of growth. I thought my life had ended; but it had only just begun. When the going got tough God would give me the boost I needed. Once when I wanted to give up, I cried to God, "It's too much. I can't do it." He gave me a dream that night. In the dream I had to walk up the side of a steep mountain. Halfway up I had to pick up barbells weighing 200 pounds, press them up over my head, and continue up the mountain. I did it! I was given strength when I needed it.

I learned how much I needed people in my life. I needed friends. Life wasn't meant to be lived in isolation. I would bear my shame and keep walking up mountains and through valleys. Miracles happened just when I needed them. I can only tell of a few. Here is one of those times I should have been taken out of the land of the living:

In 1991 I purchased a motorcycle. I rode that thing for three years and had no other transportation. I rode it rain or shine, cold or hot. I was a cyclist; mind you, not a biker. I wore a jean jacket studded with rhinestones, not a hairy chest covered with tattoos. I had trouble keeping that thing sunny side up at times, especially after my hearing impairment began January 17th of 1992, for I was losing balance. Many miracles happened in connection with that motorcycle. Here's the last, and biggest one of all.

I had just purchased a new tire and sprocket for the Honda and was riding down Berry Street on the way home. Suddenly a big Monte Carlo pulled out of a side street and broadsided the motorcycle. I saw it coming; but there was no way out. The car hit the Honda, not the other way around. My right leg should have been crushed first. But somehow the bike suddenly stopped. I think it was an Angel of the Lord who stuck his foot in front of my tire. I was thrown off the bike, flew twenty feet through the air, and landed on the pavement clear of the crash.

Coming up out of there my right heel raked the license plate along with the holder off the Monte Carlo. As I flew, all I could say was, "Ohhh shoot!"

I think it was "shoot." I remember thinking "Is this it, Lord? Am I coming home? No, I'm not flying high enough." Then I hit the pavement and rolled. No car ran over me. I propped myself up on one elbow to get a good look at that dead motorcycle, which had been demolished by the car. I said, "Shucks, I'll have to have alternate transportation now."

People started gathering around me saying, "Don't move! We've got an ambulance coming." I didn't have a scratch or a bruise. I wasn't hurt. The elderly lady who had been driving the Monte Carlo was standing looking at me and crying. She said, "I'm sorry. I hope I didn't hurt you. You're not going to die, are you?" I got up and gave her a hug; and assured her that I was okay. The ambulance pulled up and a technician started asking me questions.

What is today? What's your name? Who is the President of the United States? Who is the Vice President? I laughed and told him that I was never any good at history and told him to ask me something easier. A police officer then started talking to me. I don't know why, but I kept thinking that it was my fault. In the past everything had always been my fault. He said, "No, the lady pulled out from a side street with a stop sign. She said she didn't see you." I was happy to be practicing motorcycle safety. I wore a jean jacket even in the summer, a helmet, boots, and gloves. God has some reason for keeping me around. There is a purpose for me still.

Chapter 8
Fasting, Prayer, and Bible Reading

Many miracles happened in my life. The half cannot be told.

But this is where Bible Reading started. On July 29th of 1998 I met AS. She was in the lower atrium at church talking to a friend of mine. I needed to talk with that guy. He wanted some more copies of an article I had written called "The Power of Love" to give to friends.

I had met AS six months earlier and we didn't like each other. She had overheard me talking to a friend. He had asked about my love life. I was saying, "Yes, there's this girl who is after me; but she's so skinny and homely that I sometimes mistake her for my ironing board."

AS walked up just then and said, "It sounds like you don't have any respect for women."

I said, "All women, or just that one?" I made up my mind instantly, that's one irrational woman that I would have nothing to do with. We saw each other at times, in passing, and just greeted each other out of respect and kindness for every human being.

So, there she was, talking with my friend, and I needed to give him those articles. I walked up and interrupted long enough to hand them to him. But he started talking with me about "The Power of Love" and how it had helped several of his friends. So, I had to explain to AS what "The Power of Love" was. That was the turning point in my life. I had learned to focus on love and relinquish any fear-based thinking. I had learned to turn everything over to God for the most desirable outcome. I had learned to ask God for a change in perspective (instead of whining) to help me see every situation from His point of view. I had begun at that point to live a stress-free life.

I had experienced a miraculous healing in connection with that. In September of 1995 I had been diagnosed with Multiple Sclerosis and told that's where the hearing impairment came from. Multiple Sclerosis had done its devastating effects on my body. My body was full of pain. I had pain in every joint, and a big pain in the head. God had miraculously and instantly removed the pain at times, but it always came back to haunt me.

On February 10th of 1998 I was standing beside my bed, ready to retire for the night. My body was full of pain. I didn't want to lie down to sleep. I knew there was no position in which I would be comfortable. I wished I could sleep standing up. I was standing there talking to God. I had been reading a book called "A Return to Love" by Marianne Williamson. I had learned that my sickness and disease didn't come from God. I learned to relinquish all fear-based thinking because that is the source of disease and pain.

I said, "Father, I know now that you didn't make this pain in my body. You're not the daddy to that. It was caused by my faulty thinking. I'm sorry for blaming you for all these years. I don't know what to do to get rid of the pain. But you know exactly what will relieve it. I haven't listened very well in the past; but I'm ready to listen now. I will do whatever you suggest." Then I laid down comfortably. When I awoke the pain was still gone. And it was gone for two years.

AS said, "That sounds like something I need. I have lots of stress in my life." I told her I had another copy in the car. I asked where she was parked. She was parked on the west side of the church, and I was parked on the east side.

I said, "I'll walk you to your car; and if you'll give me a ride around to mine, I'll give you a copy."

As I was getting into her car she said, "You can move that stuff and open the window if you want."

I said, "I don't plan on sitting here that long." But I ended up sitting there for two hours. We talked a lot and got to know each other a little. I said, "You are a very interesting person." And she said the same about me. I gave her "The Power of Love" and made an appointment to talk with her some more the following Sunday after she had read the article. We met to talk the following Sunday and talked about everything else but "The Power of Love." Then I asked her to lunch. She said, "I would but I'm not eating today."

I said, "Are you fasting?" The whole church was doing a period of 40 days of prayer and fasting where people would choose a day or two for fasting.

"Yes."

"For how long will you fast?"

"I thought I would go for three days."

"Well, if you can do it I can too." So, I started right then and didn't eat for a few days. We met after the service the following Wednesday night. I asked, "Have you eaten yet?"

"No."

"How long are you going to fast?"

"I don't know. I just thought I'd fast for as long as I could.

I said to myself, "This girl is very irrational. I've got to make sure she doesn't hurt herself." So, I said, "I'm not going to eat until you do. When you decide to eat, you call me, because I'm ready."

We met after the service the following Sunday. On the previous Friday night, we were up at the church for Friday Night Coffee House. I was very hungry. I was eyeballing some crackers and grape juice that had been put out for Sunday night care groups. Someone said to me, "I don't think anyone would mind if you ate some." But, of course, I didn't. I thought about the time when King David ate the showbread.

I never fasted more than a day because when I don't eat, I get very hungry. I didn't know how to conduct a fast. The only thing I had all week was water and Tang. That's bad. Tang has sugar in it. That makes you hungrier. I was too ignorant to know that. That night AS told me that I could have V8 Juice. Wow! That was all I needed. I had plenty of nutrition then. I felt no more hunger. This could go on forever.

We met on Sunday. I asked her if she had eaten. She said, "No." I made sure she had my phone number to call me when she was ready to eat.

I said, "We can fast until we get hungry."

She said, "We can't fast 40 days."

I said, "That's what I had in mind."

Our fast lasted the full 40 days. I wanted to make it well worthwhile. So, I made a prayer list. I asked people for prayer requests. I traded lists with AS. And I began to read the Bible. I counted the chapters, 1189, and broke it down into manageable proportions. I needed to read 30 chapters a day to make it in 40 days.

By that time, I was fully dedicated to God. I had given Him all that I am and all that I have, 100%, lock stock and barrel, sinful nature and all. He can control it better than I can. I was locked into reading the Bible. That was my food for 40 days, the Word of God. ***Man shall not live on bread alone, but on every word that proceeds out of the mouth of God.*** Matthew 4:4

I was pleasantly elated. I was thrilled to be doing the fast and the Bible reading. AS and I met after the service each Sunday and Wednesday to compare notes. When we started walking toward her car it would take 45 minutes to an hour to make it because we talked so much. It seemed we would never run out of conversation topics. I was thrilled about her too. So our relationship began with 40 days of prayer and fasting.

On the 8th day she had brought her dad from a small town nearby to meet me. We went to eat together; but AS and I drank. He let me drive his car. We went to the theater with the big, curved screen and watched a movie. On the way when AS drove him back home he lectured her for the whole two hours about being with a divorced man. "You must get rid of him. You can't even be friends; it's too dangerous. If you marry a divorced man, you will lose your soul. There's got to be something drastically wrong with him if he left his family of five children, and on and on." But AS was unwilling to part with me. So, she kept me a secret.

The following Wednesday night she told me about her religious beliefs.

I've been trying for eight years now to help her look at that in a different light. I have also done the fasting, prayer, and Bible reading for eight years and this is the ninth. AS and I have fasted together for at least five years. Others have joined us over the years. Some do a juice fast, like we do. Some fast from meat and eat fruit and vegetables only. Some fast from TV. I am the only one who does the Bible reading. I haven't been able to interest others in taking the time to do that. It only takes two or three hours a day. We all have twenty-four hours to use as we please. I just don't watch TV. I haven't done that in seventeen years. Life is so wonderful without it! And I dedicated everything to God including my time. He portions it out better than I can. There's time for everything. There's money for everything. I have no wants, and I have no desires. I have no debt. Nobody owns me but God.

In our fifth year together AS decided to let me go so she could be free to go take care of her aged parents. We had been everywhere together and done everything (spiritually upright things) but she said we were never anything, that we never had a relationship. What did we have then? I wondered.

God gave me perfect peace about the situation. From that day on a girl breaking off the relationship has never hurt me. I used to be emotionally tortured. I would be distraught for days, weeks, maybe months. But now I just put every girl and every situation in the hands of God. If we don't make it, it wasn't meant to be, and it wasn't God's will. I am a very valuable person, and so is AS. God is our Father. He wants His children to have happiness. He always has our best interests in mind.

Trouble is, I'm still single today, seventeen years after the break-up of my marriage. But I'm very happy to be living alone. When I retreat to my haven of rest I have perfect peace. I have lots of friends. Even AS is back in my life again. All her plans to cover up her tracks backfired. Now her father is gone, and her mother's mind is changed about divorced men. She loves me and wants me to visit and eat with them every day. She is convinced that it would be okay for us to marry. I think I'll just keep my peace. Marriage doesn't hold such a big attraction to me anymore.

Sections were removed from this page to honor AS. I had written some things that proved to be disturbing and degrading to her. Without AS this book could not have been written. She is the one who led me to a godlier life and to intimacy with God.

Chapter 9
How we conducted the Fast

40 Days of Fasting, Prayer, and Bible Reading Aug.1st to Sept.9th

During these 40 days we will consume only juices. You'll get plenty of nutrition only in the liquid form. V8 juice gives you plenty of energy and has all the nutrients you can get out of vegetables. Orange, Grapefruit, apple, and Grape juices are very good in any combination. Drink Lemon juice with water and Maple syrup, with a little Cayenne pepper, for helping cleanse the body's interior. Always drink plenty of water. Avoid sugar. Liquefied (seedless) watermelon is a good source of protein & a tasty drink to enjoy.

Benefits of this experience:

Physical:

You will experience a complete cleansing of your system.

Pain you may be experiencing now will disappear.

You will relinquish adipose tissue at the rate of 1pound per day (You'll lose weight).

You'll build endurance. (If you can control your appetite, you can control anything!)

You'll beat the August heat. (You'll feel calm and cool much of the time.)

You'll have increased energy & feel livelier (but take it easy & conserve it)

Spiritual:

You'll feel very close to God.

You'll feel peaceful, calm, and serene.

You'll gain a better understanding of the whole Bible story, reading through like a novel

Miracles will happen - praying for each other.

Your whole day will be a prayer and worship to God.

You'll have more time for the Bible reading when you're not eating.

Make a prayer list and start each morning with prayer. List all the people you work with and Bible study with; and talk to each one and get specific prayer requests. You'll be delighted with the results of this experience!

On September 9th we can meet at Souper Salad to eat (We must begin with soup and gradually get the digestive system working hard again so we don't overload it)

Chapter 10
The Bible Reading Schedule

The Old Testament in 31 Days (929 chapters)

Aug. 1 – Genesis 1-30

Aug. 2 – Genesis 31-50, Exodus 1-10

Aug. 3 – Exodus 11-40

Aug. 4 – Leviticus 1-27, Numbers 1-3

Aug. 5 – Numbers 4-33

Aug. 6 – Numbers 34-36, Deuteronomy 1-27

Aug. 7 – Deuteronomy 28-34, Joshua 1-23

Aug. 8 – Joshua 24, Judges 1-21, Ruth 1-4, I Sam 1-4

Aug. 9 – I Samuel 5-31, II Samuel 1-3

Aug. 10 – II Samuel 4-24, I Kings 1-9

Aug. 11 – I Kings 10-22, II Kings 1-17

Aug. 12 – II Kings 18-25, I Chronicles 1-22

Aug. 13 – I Chronicles 23-29, II Chronicles 1-23

Aug. 14 – II Chron 24-36, Ezra 1-10, Nehemiah 1-7

Aug. 15 – Nehemiah 8-13, Esther 1-10, Job 1-14

Aug. 16 – Job 15-42, Psalms 1-2

Aug. 17 – Psalms 3-32

Aug. 18 – Psalms 33-62

Aug. 19 – Psalms 63-92

Aug. 20 – Psalms 93-122

Psalm 118:8 is the exact center of the Bible It is better to take refuge in the Lord than to trust in man

Aug. 21 – Psalms 123-150, Proverbs 1-2

Aug. 22 – Proverbs 3-31, Ecclesiastes 1

Aug. 23 – Eccl 2-12, Song of Sol 1-8, Isaiah 1-11 -

Aug. 24 – Isaiah 12-41

Aug. 25 – Isaiah 42-66, Jeremiah 1-5

Aug. 26 – Jeremiah 6-36

Aug. 27 – Jeremiah 37-52, Lam 1-5, Ezekiel 1-10

Aug. 28 – Ezekiel 11-41

Aug. 29 – Ezekiel 42-48, Daniel 1-12, Hosea 1-11

Aug. 30 – Hosea 12-14, Joel 1-3, Amos 1-9, Obadiah 1, Jonah 1-4, Micah 1-7, Nahum 1-3

Aug. 31 – Habakkuk 1-3, Zephaniah 1-3, Haggai 1-2, Zechariah 1-14, Malachi 1-4

The New Testament in 9 Days (260 chapters)

Sept. 1 - Matthew 1-28, Mark 1-2

Sept. 2 - Mark 3-16, Luke 1-16

Sept. 3 – Luke 17-24, John 1-21

Sept. 4 – Acts 1-28, Romans 1-2

Sept. 5 – Romans 3-16, I Corinthians 1-16

Sept. 6 – II Corinthians 1-13, Galatians 1-6, Ephesians 1-6, Philippians 1-4

Sept. 7 –Colossians 1-4, I Thessalonians 1-5, II Thessalonians 1-3, I Timothy 1-6, II Timothy 1-4

Sept. 8 – Titus 1, Philemon 1, Hebrews 1-13, James 1-5, I Peter 1-5, II Peter 1-3

Sept. 9 – I John 1-5, II John 1, III John 1, Jude 1, Revelations 1-22

Chapter 11
What is Happening in my Life?

Every year after the fast, several of us met at Souper Salad and began with soup to go back to eating. Hunger was never an issue. We could have gone without eating for many more days. But one always has to wonder what it's doing to the digestive system. And losing too much weight makes one unattractive. I would just turn control over to God and trust Him to let me know if I should go back to eating.

For seven years I did the 40-day fast from August 1st to September 9th on the seventh year God gave me rest from my labors. I retired at age forty-eight. This is how it happened: I have Multiple Sclerosis, that's what the doctors say. I never believed it. That's just one of many names given to a condition in the body that isn't fully understood and isn't likely to go away. I know exactly what caused my condition; and I know what relieves it. The route to retirement began with a lamb chop.

A New Zealand Lamb Chop

After the fast of 2003 we had a cookout at my place, just as we did every year, to celebrate God's blessings and miracles that happened during the fasting and praying. After the cookout I developed a bladder infection that affected my whole body. I thought it was a third-world disease from eating the "New Zealand Lamb Chop." We had roasted two lamb legs over a campfire. The lamb legs came from New Zealand.

A few days after the cookout my health crashed at work. I barely made it home with lots of pain in every joint. I had to sleep in the truck for a while before I could even drive because of the pain in my head. This was not an unusual part of my Multiple Sclerosis symptoms. But all the pain in my body went away every fast and usually didn't come back until many days after I had gone back to eating. Now this had come back early.

After I arrived home that day, I was paralyzed from the waist down for the next twenty-four hours. I took a couple days off work to recuperate. I had been working in the hot sun. Extreme heat or extreme cold always does me in. So, I had to refuse to work out there anymore. Work coming into the shop was slow, so my boss directed me to do repairs and painting on the building. He put another man on it, and that guy quit completely. Then I didn't feel so bad about refusing to do it.

A Puzzling Dream

A couple days later I had a dream. In the dream it was ten days until the destruction of the United States. I woke up puzzled as to what the dream meant. And God said, "I want you to live like there is only a short time left."

In a couple more days I was laid off from my job. God had told me that morning that I would be laid off. My boss waited until nearly 4:00 to tell me. He had a very hard time getting it out. I had been his best employee for 24 years. I knew what he was trying to say, but I didn't rush him. I waited patiently. I had no hard feelings and no worries. I was excited, wondering what God was leading me into next, besides there was only a short time left. When my boss finally got the words out, I shook his hand and said, "Robert, you have been a good man to work for these 24 years."

He said in almost a whisper, "Well, what are you going to do now?"

I said, "I don't know. I can't get another job the way my health is. I have written a few books. I'm going to try and get them published. There's enough money in the bank to keep me going for a couple of months. I'll just see what happens. God is leading me into something."

I didn't know what would happen. But I knew what the Lord had told me, "I want you to live like there is only a short time left." I would never quit my job. I would have died amid building furniture. Then I would have been buried at Wal-Mart so that AS would come visit me often. (She spends a lot of time there.)

God had rescued me. I needed a break. I worked very hard for thirty-six years beginning at age twelve. And I didn't quit when I came home in the evenings either. I worked on the house and yard until dark. Then I slept very soundly until 4:00am and got up to do it all over again. Nothing is like work to me. Everything is fun. I work with God at my side. And I sleep very well at night.

Immediately friends started telling me to apply for Unemployment. I had never been off work before. I had no idea how to do things like that. I found a way to apply on the Internet. It was so easy. They were about to send me money immediately. My boss had told me that I could apply if I wanted to, but that it would cost him a higher quarterly premium. I just barely got the Unemployment stopped before they could send me the first check. I decided I couldn't do that because I wasn't going to be applying for jobs. That was the only condition for Unemployment. Apply for one job a week.

That would have been deception. I couldn't offer any employer a healthy man who could put in a full week's work.

The day before I got laid off that Monday, a friend had asked me to come and refinish his front door. That same Sunday a girl had asked me to fix the burnt up electric wire going to her air-conditioner. I had worked hard for six hours, with a headache, and spent $50.00 to do that for her. The Lord had blessed her majestically and kept the house from burning down in an electrical fire that she caused by sticking a screwdriver into the electrical controls; but still she saw fit to cancel the check and beat me out of the money. She said she couldn't really afford that. She said I had charged her too much. And she had to help her husband get out of jail for he had been incarcerated on a "trumped up charge."

She said she would give it back to me when she got back on her feet. I said, "Listen, it's okay. You don't have to pay anything. I'm happy to have done that for you." To this day I am her enemy. She said, "You deserved to get laid off your job after trying to charge me so much." The Lord would have blessed her so much more. But she chose her blessing, a little $235.00. It was okay. God gave it to her. But had she done what was right, her blessing would have been so much more. My blessing was magnanimous.

Took the Fast Way Down

I refinished my friend's front door; and immediately I had another one to do. I put a sign on the back of my truck and got a few more jobs. Now here comes another miracle. While I did the second door, I also worked for another friend on his roof, which was so steep I had to have a rope to hold me in place along with footholds. God directed me to buy a hundred-foot rope, when I was going to get the fifty-foot one. I connected it around the chimney and had clips attached to me like a mountain climber. I needed the full hundred feet.

I did the whole job without incident, until I got to the last row of ridge caps. Then I climbed the ladder with an arm full of ridge caps. I had to grab the rope and pull myself up onto the roof because it was too steep to step off the top of the ladder. As I stepped onto the roof, the rope stretched, I lost my balance and stepped over the edge.

I fell two stories, twenty feet, landed on my bony bottom, fell backward, and bumped the back of my head solidly against the cement slab that holds the air-conditioner. I had no injuries. I was up crawling around on my hand and knees and checking myself over; and I was talking to God. I said, "I hope this doesn't mean I'm going to have brain damage. I've got to use that thing for the rest of my life."

And a voice answered me. It said, "Are you alright?" It was the owner of the place. He had come running out when he heard the crash because I had taken out a window on the way down. The back of my shirt was torn all the way across the shoulders, and the arm was ripped at the right bicep. But I had no cuts, bruises, scratches, or pain anywhere. I have no explanation except that God helped me. He is keeping me around for something. In all this I'm still excited about what God is leading me into next. And I'm still wondering about what the ten days in the dream meant.

Jehovah Jireh Provides

Many miracles happened during the ten months I was without an income. God took care of everything. No bills ever got behind. My expenses were $1600 a month; and it all came from somewhere every month. Many of my Christian brothers and sisters helped me, some by purchasing merchandise I was selling.

When I was given much there was no excess; when I was given little there was no lack. I worked wherever I could for two months until my health gave in entirely. Then when I couldn't do anything, I was at the computer every waking moment trying to establish an income. I never slacked off for a minute. Stress did begin to eat at me when I had no idea where the next month's payments would come from, and pain and disability were so intense. But I kept submitting myself to God. Once a friend at church asked me how things were going. I said, "Adversity is very strong; but I think there is hope for the future." Her eyes watered.

I had been remodeling a house for a Toastmaster friend, doing that every evening after any other work during the day. I had started that a few months before I got laid off my job. One night coming home from that job, and from getting material for Blessing Boxes, which I was making and selling, I was driving down the freeway and my health crashed. I could go no more. God quickly ushered me off the freeway and a few blocks to a friend's house. I knocked on his door and after we greeted each other warmly I said, "Can I lie down for a few minutes? I'm very sick." Breathing stains and lacquer had done me in.

He and his wife revived me and nursed me back to health. His wife, who is a nurse took my vitals and told me that my blood pressure had skyrocketed. She had never seen blood pressure so high. I don't remember the specifics of what the pressure was. I don't understand that stuff anyway. I wasn't even concerned. But she made me promise to go see a doctor the next day and go apply for Disability Benefits.

As I was driving over to the Social Security Administration Office I kept thinking about my dad. He had been on Disability or Welfare all his life; and he wasn't nice to us. He was very abusive. I was reliving those childhood experiences, and when I arrived at the office, I barely dragged myself to the door; and it was locked. I was nine minutes too late, and I was relieved because I didn't want to apply for Disability. When I arrived home, I was in so much pain that all I could do was lie on the couch. I experienced another 24 hours of paralysis from the waist down. I slept in that spot for the night. I really thought I would never wake up again. I jotted down my funeral wishes; then I submitted myself to God and told Him to do with me whatever He would.

In mid-January, I finally made it to apply for Disability. I had to do something. My body wouldn't go any more. I had finished remodeling the girl's house; but she beat me out of the $3500.00 I was to get at the completion of the job. She refinanced the house, got $75,000.00, then let it go back to the mortgage company; and declared bankruptcy. She loved the work I did. It was top notch all the way. But she loved money more than honesty and fairness. I filed a lean on the house, turned the situation over to God, and didn't worry about it. I had no hard feelings; after all there was only a short time left.

I had applied for Supplemental Security Income too; but that was refused. I said to myself, and to everyone else, "That is probably a blessing." And it was!

The first thing I said to those people when I entered the office was this: There were dozens of people still waiting. I took a number and had someone listen for my number. I walked up to the counter and the girl looked so worn out. I wanted to cheer her up, so I said, "Do all these people want money from the Government?"

She said, "Wellll, yes."

I said, "I want to make a donation!"

The last thing I said to them after my interview was, "I will never be disabled! As long as I have a brain to think, there is something I can do to make a living." They probably wrote in the report, "Mentally incapacitated too."

I didn't depend on getting Disability. There was nothing I could do to convince anyone that I was disabled. I looked fine, and I still do. If they had seen me the first time I came to that office, they would have given it to me instantly. I just kept busy every waking moment trying to establish an income. I have many talents. I must figure out how to market them. I was just learning about the Internet. I just got online September 13th of 2002. I'm not skilled in the ways of the world.

I was trying to sell the products of my talents on the Internet and through e-mail marketing. The only email addresses I had were my church friends'. Between Thanksgiving and Christmas of 2003, I sold $900.00 worth of Blessing Boxes and introduced people to the idea of jotting down their blessings each time, storing them in the box, and opening the box on Thanksgiving Day to thank God for all their blessings.

Miracles continued: Toward the end of December a friend emailed and said, "I want to make your house payment. Where can we meet?" We met at the Kroger store and he gave me $750.00. He tried to make other payments for me at times, even more house payments, but each time I had to tell him, "All the bills are paid right now, let's just wait and see what happens." I never asked anyone for money; I just kept trying to sell the products of my talents. I really wanted to get speaking and teaching memory going.

In March of 2004 a couple guys from church got impatient with me. They took it upon themselves to convince me that I needed to get a job. Despite my hearing impairment and my ill health, I was doing all I could to make a living. I could not represent myself to any employer as a man healthy enough to work even part time. They tried to convince me to apply for Unemployment. I wouldn't do that because it was dishonest. On the one hand I would have been putting in applications saying to employers that I could work a full day or a week; and on the other hand, I was saying to the Social Security Administration that I'm disabled to work. I would never do that. I would die first before I would lie. They said, "You can't depend on getting Disability. They're going to automatically refuse you the first time you apply. It could take a couple of years. You can't make that happen."

I said, "I know that I can't make it happen. But God can! He knows my condition. And this meeting was not from God. I'm going to go to other churches for a while. I can't show my face here right now. I will look sad, and people will feel sorry for me."

He said, "That's crazy, you can't walk into a new church and expect them to support you when they don't even know you."

I said, "I have not asked anyone for money except the Brother's Keeper program has made the last couple house payments. I'm not going to ask any church for money. God is not limited to providing for me through a church. And I don't see how it matters; you just cut me off of all church support here." It wasn't the whole church doing that. It was one man's idea.

During the month of April 2004 money and support came from everywhere. Some of it was very surprising. There were some from my church who wanted to help. I gently told them to wait and see what happened. The funniest one was this: In January my roof fell in. I was delighted. Now I am just like Job. I said, "I hope God still treats people like He did Job, because Satan surely does." God had prompted me to report it to my insurance company. They sent out an engineer to prove that it happened slowly over time. I said, "Yeah really, the roof just eased itself down and rested on its laurels like a sway-back nag."

In April, they sent me a letter saying that they could not cover this claim. We won't be paying anything for it. But we advise you to fix it before it gets worse. A week later I received a check for $400.00 from that insurance company along with a little note that said you better cash this quickly. I said, "No problem!"

On May 11th, slightly over 30 days from the meeting with those two guys, and a couple weeks less than four months from the time I had applied for Disability, I received the Determination, "We have found you to be disabled according to our rules."

A week earlier, at a friend's advice, I had visited my former employer to see what my chances were of getting my 401k Profit Sharing. I hadn't even thought about that before. I knew there was no way of getting it until age 65 and it was slowly dwindling away over the years with loses. The secretary said, "When you get that Disability Determination, bring it to me and I'll see that you get your Profit-Sharing money."

Remember when they refused me the Supplemental Security Income? I said, "That's probably a blessing." It was! God is in control! Had I received the okay for that, it would have been an instant $910.00 a month, but I would not have gotten the Disability Determination. If I had not received the Disability Determination I would not have been eligible for my retirement Profit Sharing. And the Disability was more than twice as much.

For the next few weeks, I went from one financial advisor to another trying to decide what was best to do with $140,000.00. That's quite a change from almost a minute ago. That's how God works when you let Him have control. I had never dreamed that could happen. I paid off my house, my burial policy, bought new computer equipment, and invested $100,000.00. Now I live with no bills but utilities; and I'm working on my future. I will take another distribution in 2011 to buy a new car. That is one of the biggest blessings of my life, one that everyone wants, not to have to work our lives away. I dedicated my time to God and He has given me back all the time I used to spend working for a living. I don't mean to be bragging about these dollar amounts or inviting charities to bombard me with requests for help. But it's so much more impressive to know the far-reaching extent of what God will do for His children.

I know we don't earn God's blessings. But I think we are rewarded for giving kindness and blessing to others; and for dedicating everything we are to God. During the fast of 2003 I gave $100.00 to a girl with cancer to help her out with expenses while she had no income. Prior to that, I had donated $100.00 to a single mom who was having difficulty. Those two I never met. I was in the habit of blessing others with $100.00 at a time because once in 1996 when I was about $75.00 short of meeting my expenses a guy from my singles group walked up and handed me a 100-dollar bill. He said, "God told me you would be needing this."

Since then, I have given away many 100-dollar bills. During my ten months without an income, I found opportunity to bless others at times. I gave away several of the Blessing Boxes as well as other things. And for the last ten years I have put all the money that I make through my Presenting memorized documents and Teaching memory techniques, and all my extra money into an account that I call God's account. And I use it for God's purposes only, namely, to bless others.

Now, do you think all that is a big blessing? Listen to this: Before I ever received the first Disability Benefit check the biggest part of my ailments was removed from me. I'm not saying that I no longer qualify. The Social Security Administration says I automatically qualify now and have been given permanent Disability because of my hearing impairment. I don't have much balance because of it. I take a lot of falls. I'm especially out of balance when I get tired. But all that disability that had plagued me for ten months was relieved by one great big dose of involuntary bee sting therapy.

A swarm of bees landed on my mustache and stung it all at one time, one great big sting. Only God could orchestrate that. That's a wonderful story too. But I can't fit everything in. I still want to describe my prayer sessions and tell you a couple of fabulous things that happened in connection with that, one of them is so unusual and different than anything I ever experienced that it can't be beaten.

Now, do you remember the dream I had about the destruction of the United States, and how I had puzzled about what the ten days meant? Listen to these significant tens: It was ten days from the fast of 2003 to the cookout we had to celebrate answered prayer and the blessings of God. It was ten more days until the layoff from my job. It was ten months from the loss of one income to the beginning of the other. And it was ten days from the beginning of the new income to the next fast, which was the 7th and the last fast for me. This year I'm just fasting from "sin," because my preacher is against it.

Chapter 12
An Angel on Earth

Backing up a little let me tell you this: All through the fast of 2003, which was the 6th year we did this, a beautiful young lady from my singles group took it upon herself to feed me with encouragement every day. And boy oh boy, I really needed it too. I was experiencing many trials and tribulations, and even persecution. She was one of God's Angels on Earth led by the Spirit to minister to me. Let's just call her JP Justifiably Perfect. She said that now she'd like to be called JS Joyfully Saved. I gave her a special email address to use for me; and my name was Jac, which are the initials of my pseudonym.

Very early in the fast of 2003 I received some persecution from a man who says, "Me and God are like this" crossing his fingers. Do you know that persecution only comes from other Christians? Non-believers don't care about the seemingly silly things Christians do. They don't give us any trouble. But some other Christians want everyone to believe like they do. And they make trouble at times if you won't conform to their beliefs. "Me and God" that is an example of not putting God first.

I was working away from the shop, remodeling the office space of my boss's mini warehouses. I would do my Bible reading at break time and lunchtime; and I would be drinking my V8 Juice while I read. Mr. "MeAnGod" worked at that office. He knew about my fasting because I had sent out emails soliciting prayer requests; and he received one but didn't send any prayer requests.

So, while I was reading, he would come in and start blasting away at me saying that I was doing wrong. He said, "me and God are like this, crossing his fingers, and when God tells me something to tell you; you better listen. And He told me to tell you not to read the Old Testament, get in the New Testament; and don't fast more than a day or two. You think you're so spiritual reading the Bible at work. You are just nothing. I am the one who is close to God. He saved my life once; and He gave me a vision of Heaven and hell."

Wow, that was heavy stuff. I said, "God speaks to you about you, and to me about me. And if He wanted me to quit fasting, I think He would have told me six years ago. And if He wanted me to stay out of the Old Testament, He would tell me so."

He said, "You think you know so much about the Bible, did you know that Noah built an ark?"

"Yes, I do; and do you know who the first Judge in Israel was?"

He said, "No." And with many more words he was really getting adamant. He was coming down on me like a wolf on the fold. It was a little too much to take on an empty stomach.

I said, "It sounds like you remember the bedtime stories we used to get as children and not much more about the Bible. Now if you will excuse me, I have to get back to work."

I emailed JP and told her about it that night. She emailed me back and just filled me with encouragement. The subject line, which I had applied to my note to her said, **do not be discouraged by the onslaught of the wicked**. Praise the Lord!! Blessed are you when men persecute you for my name's sake. Satan must really consider you a threat. He wants you to stop so badly that he has stirred up someone to come against you. I'd say you are highly honored! Glory to God and keep up the good work, Mighty Prayer Warrior!

JP had started giving me encouragement way before the fast, all during the fast, and continued after the fast when I lost my job. She stuck with me all through my ten-month saga. Without her blessings it would have been much harder for me. All during that fast, at the end of each email, we would pronounce blessings on each other. You can really bless people with scripture; but you can pronounce heavy curses too. Let me give you just a few of the blessings we pronounced on each other.

From JP: May you be flooded with blessings from our Father; and may you receive divine health from Jehovah Rapha. May you grow in grace and knowledge of our Lord and Savior, Jesus Christ. May your life be renewed, your zeal increase, and your devotion taken to new heights. May you have "joy unspeakable and full of glory" (as the Word says).

From JP: May the glorious God of Heaven be glorified in all your praises, your fast, and your life. May you be touched by His glorious presence in new and special ways.

From JP: Rather than a blessing, a reminder: You have the full reserve of God's power abiding in you. And nothing is too difficult for God. That means you are a powerhouse! Believe it, receive it, achieve it. You really can do all things through Christ who strengthens you. And this is the victory that overcomes the world, even our faith.

From JP: I pray that you will reap so many return blessings from all that you are giving out. I pray that God will cause you to triumph over your enemies (persecutors). I pray that you will be completely healed and whole. I pray that you will have such joy and peace that you feel absolutely, undeniably fantastic! I pray that you will lack for nothing. I pray that the joy of the Lord is your strength, now and always. May the light of the Lord's glorious countenance fill every particle of your being. In His love & light, JP

From JP: Speaking of my memorizing and presenting: You go, guy! You have a special and unique calling which really shouldn't be so unique. I think a lot more of us should tap into special things God wants us to do, like you're doing, but we don't take the time and effort. I know I don't. I speak this to the shame of so many Christians, including myself. I have known this for a long time though. We probably all have our excuses. At any rate, I just want to encourage you that what you are doing is important and impressive. You go the extra mile, and you pay the price to do what God lays on your heart to do. I truly believe there will be a special crown for you in Heaven. And it will be worth it all then!

From Jac: Now may the Lord shine down on you so bright and so warm you will tingle all over. May the lesser lights of the night, which so beautify the Celestial Ballroom, twinkle in your eyes and gleam from your smile. Let starshine splash your face. Let the light of the Son of God, which is so delightfully thrilling, illumine everything upon which your gaze chances to rest. Let the mountains jump for joy, and the rivers clap their hands. Let the seas roar, the oceans wave, and the rocks cry out. Let the Lord be praised! May He inhabit your praises, fill His holy temple in your heart, and make you sing for joy. Lay your precious head to rest softly in His arms. Dream with the Angels as their wings spread over you protecting you from all harm.

From Jac: Now may God cause you to drink from the river of His delights and give you the desires of your heart because you delight in Him. I pray you will cease striving and know that He is God that He sits on His holy throne and is highly exalted. Recognize that He is so gracious to you according to His loving-kindness that He causes your soul to abide in prosperity. Do not fear in the days of adversity when man has trampled on you, for He will lift you up. He puts all your tears in His little bottle. Angels cry with you when you are hurt and rejoice with you when your heart is made glad. God will count no sin against you for the precious blood of Jesus has covered them all. You will walk with uprightness of heart all of your days. The enemy cannot harm you. You are blessed of the Lord!

From Jac: Now may the Lord brighten the heavens as He arrives on a lightning bolt, His thunderous voice awakening every living soul. Even so, in Heaven He still sits on His holy throne. Let all flesh and spirit keep silence before the Majesty of Heaven. He is looking at us as His eyes roam to and fro about the earth seeking to uphold those whose hearts are completely His. Let Him who searches the hearts examine and know that you are completely His. And whom He foreknew He also predestined to become conformed to the image of His Son. He is conforming you to Christ, and He is conforming me too. Have patience with me as God does. Thank you for your message.

From Jac: Now I pray that the eyes of your heart may be opened to see His Angels surrounding you every minute and rejoicing with you every time you triumph over the various trials in your life that crop up to plague you. I pray that you may have a full understanding and awareness of His love that is so great for you, and for all of us, that He longs to share His blessings with us abundantly, and yearns for us to be of such a heart and mind to receive them. I pray that today you will be blessed exceedingly beyond all that you can dream or imagine, that your feelings will soar in such ecstasy you can hardly contain them as you bathe in the Sonlight of His love. The eyes of the Lord roam to and fro about the earth seeking to uphold those whose hearts are completely His. Your heart is surely centered on Him. I pray that He will bless you with the desires of your heart, make all your tough challenges come out so joyful it will tickle you pink, and touch your mind with the depths of His wisdom to add to the marvelous spiritual intelligence you already possess. It is my hope that God will fully enrich your life, fulfill your hopes and dreams beyond all that you can imagine, and fill you so full of the warmth of His love that it comes bubbling out to bless all those around you. With brotherly love! You **are** more so Jesus! I love your godliness and your intelligence. You are a wonderful friend. I never want to lose you. I hope this friendship is forever!

From Jac: And now I hope for every blessing for you that you have pronounced for me. The eyes of the Lord are upon you because your heart is completely His. He will make everything in your life work together for good because you love Him. He will cause you to drink from the river of His delights. He will establish you in all your ways. The enemy cannot touch you because God's Angels are all around you. Rest assured, in the arms of God, that no harm will befall you. The Majesty of

Heaven sits on His throne in magnificent glory. Peace be to you!

And there were other blessings pronounced. That alone would have caused my heart to soar. But the notes of encouragement were even more fabulous. I never had such a wonderful experience in my life. It was totally from God. He prompted JP to do it. This was not a romantic thing. I knew she was engaged to be married, and now she is. But her words and expressions of care and concern carried me to the top of a very high mountain; and I soared high above it on the clouds.

Through all that, and because of God's blessings, I learned to love trials and tribulation. I know the "Power of TnT" and I'm going to write a book about it sometime. I told God time and time again how I love them. Then after the fast of 2003 I got to experience one of the biggest trials of my life. God used that and other things to prepare me for what was about to happen. During that sixth fast the most amazing things happened. Let me tell you some of the things that showed that God was in favor of each fasting experience.

Chapter 13
When God is in it, you know it

Some very wonderful things happened during every fast; but let me just mention a few things that showed me that God was in favor of them. This happened as soon as I woke up on the first day of the fast of either 2001 or 2002. When it's time to get up in the morning I don't procrastinate. When that alarm goes off at 4:00am I immediately throw one leg over the side; and if nothing grabs it, I throw the other one over and I'm up! So, the alarm goes off at 4:00am, I feel so excited about getting a new fast started, I throw one leg over the side, and immediately God said, "Start with praise!"

Wow! Then I was even more excited! Can you think of a better way for God to tell me that He is right there with me? At the beginning of that year's fast, my praise sessions grew tremendously. I would praise for an hour or two before even getting into prayer and supplication. It's easy to praise for over an hour if you use some of my tactics. I have a list of 18 names of God that I locked into memory many years ago; and I dearly love to praise Him by all of those names. I will make the list here for you:

INTIMACY WITH GOD AND MY WELL-WORN BIBLE

Names of God that Describe His character

1. **Father**–Matthew 6:9 says we can call Him our Father who art in Heaven
2. **Elohiem**–Almighty creator, unlimited strength, nothing is too difficult for Him
3. **Jehovah**–The existing one, the great I Am, who always was and always will be
4. **El Elyon**–God most high
5. **Adonai**–Lord and Master
6. **El Roi**–The God who sees
7. **El Shaddai**–Almighty God, sufficient strength, the comforter, the breasted one
8. **El Olam**–Everlasting, changeless, the same yesterday- today- and forever
9. **Jehovah Jireh**–Our provider
10. **Jehovah Psidcanue**-The Lord our righteousness, the absolute standard
11. **Jehovah Rapha**–The Lord our healer
12. **Jehovah Nissi**–Our banner and our victory
13. **Jehovah Quanna**–A jealous God
14. **Jehovah Mekeddish**–The Lord our sanctifier
15. **Jehovah Shalom**–The Lord our peace
16. **Jehovah Sabaoth**–The Lord of hosts
17. **Jehovah Rohi**–The Lord our shepherd
18. **Jehovah Shammah**–The God who is always there

So, I would praise Him by each one of these names, quoting the meaning of the name and adding to it whatever came to mind; then telling Him what that means to my life.

That would take about an hour. Then I would present to Him a few poems I wrote to Him years ago. I have a poem book with 82 poems called "Poetic Reflections." If I still wanted to praise more, I would read to Him some of the most wonderful Psalms of praise that David wrote.

Then I would finally get to my prayer list. I had always collected prayer requests from friends. And I would have a long list, hundreds of people. But sometimes I felt bad about myself, and I couldn't talk to people in person so I would try to get requests through the email.

I would get specific requests and list them beside each of the names. Now this is how to get through the list quick: I begin with a general prayer for everyone, asking for the most wonderful blessings according to His riches in glory in Christ Jesus. I can assure you that does not mean gold and silver either. I would always ask for God's will to be done in each life. I would ask for God to draw their hearts to Himself, for each one to be fully dedicated to Him. That God would care for whatever is most prominent in each life. And I pray for many other things. Then I lift each person up to God by name and silently read (think it to God) the prayer request listed for each one. I never tell God how to answer anyone's prayer request, and I don't suggest ways for Him to take care of any of His children. He knows what He will do for each one. I think that you would not get an answer when you try to tell God what to do.

Chapter 14
The Alpha and the Omega

Something so special happened in the fast of 2003 that now all my prayers begin and end with God. This is what happened:

On Saturday August 16th I got up at 4:00am and began with praise. I praised for three hours then began praying and supplicating. I was praying so earnestly for several people that tears were pouring out of my eyes. I was so deep into the praying (a long way into the praise) that I lost all sense of self or where I was or what I was doing. My spirit was melded with God's Spirit. The prayers took another hour and when I finally came to the end of the list the Spirit moved me to keep on praying. And I found myself praying for God.

Now I know that nobody prays for God. It's insane thinking to believe that my prayers for God could achieve anything at all. But when God leads me, through His Spirit, to do something, I obey without question. I was sobbing profusely from the very beginning because I had a hard time getting prayer requests that year; and God gave me His. By the 16th I had a whole four pages of them because I went around asking people at church. I had at first tried to get prayer requests through the email; and I got very few answers. I felt bad thinking that no one counted my prayers worth anything; then God asked me to pray for Him. I sobbed convulsively so much that I had a hard time praying.

I said, "Wow! Father, it's an honor to pray for you; but I can't imagine you having any needs."

He said, "Yes, I do have needs. I need the loyalty and devotion of my children. I need the praise that comes from devoted hearts. I need to be able to call upon any one of my children at any given moment and expect to encounter a willing mind."

And He said other things; I can't remember all of it right now.

So, I began to pray for Him, "Father, I lift you to the highest place in my life, to the highest place in the whole universe; and I pray that you will be blessed today far above and beyond that with which you have blessed any man. I pray that your blessings will return to you a hundred-fold. I pray that you will bless yourself for your goodness; for all that you do for so many, for the way that you unselfishly serve us and answer our prayers. I pray that all of your children will bless you by dedicating their lives to you. I pray that each one will become 100% yours, all that they are and all that they have. I pray that your needs will be met abundantly. I pray that your joy will be magnified and your pain diminished. I pray that the joy you feel when we do good will far exceed the pain that you feel when we do wrong or the pain you experience while empathizing with our hurts. I pray that nothing that is against you will stand, that all of your enemies will fall. I pray that your will be done on Earth just as it is done in Heaven, without hesitation, without question.

And I prayed many more things, with beautiful words from the Psalms, with tears pouring out of my eyes constantly. This prayer is more like what I pray every day than what I prayed then, because the Spirit was wording the prayer and I don't remember everything from three years ago. It was such a moving experience that my heart was mellowed out; and I was floating comfortably on the clouds above the highest mountain for days.

As soon as I told my best friend at work about it, he blasted me away with very harsh criticism for my foolishness and arrogance. So, you can think what you will, I'm just telling it like it happened. It's just like my Father to do that for me because I'm the least in the Kingdom. But the encourager God appointed for me during that fast built me up like I was the greatest spiritual giant. I loved it! And I love her forever, even though I haven't heard from her in a couple years. That makes it even more amazing to me. She was given the assignment for a little while when it was needed, but not forever.

I pronounced a curse on the fellow employee who had blasted me, and on Mr. "MeAnGod." I pronounced the curse using scripture. It was as powerful as the blessings that JP and I pronounced for each other. But I repented and never gave them the written curse. They were in my old computer. When I bought new computer equipment and backed up all the programs and files in the old one, I lost 50% of my files and all pictures in the transfer. So those curses were buried, and so were many of my writings and pictures I was saving. I lost the first "Intimacy with God" I had written. It was over 10,000 words, and only about half done. Now I think this one is much better. I'm a different person writing it because God has done more work on conforming me to the image of His son. This is over 34,000 words, three times as long as Romans.

Chapter 15
The Blessings of Bible Reading

After hearing all that has happened in my life because of Bible reading, along with the prayer and fasting, everyone should want to just do it. But to some it's an overwhelming thing to think of reading the whole Bible. It's a big book! I know when I first looked into the Bible, back when I was nineteen, I was like too confused to even know where to begin. It was a King James Version; and I couldn't understand anything anyway.

This is the cutest thing I've ever heard about the overwhelming size of the Bible. Recently, I was telling a small group of people about some of God's wondrous works in my life. And I mentioned that I'm reading the Bible completely through right now and recording the time it takes to read it. I said, "I started on August 1st." And one girl said, "Last year!" It was also her idea to conduct the Bible Reading Contest.

When a full Bible is an overwhelming thought the mind tends to want to promote the Bible reading schedules where you can read it in bits and pieces in one year. I've done that before when I was a baby Christian. I didn't get much out of it, at least not nearly as much as I get out of it reading straight through like a novel. That way you get the whole picture running through like a movie. Would you get much out of jumping around from scene to scene at random in a movie? Would you get much out of jumping from front to back and getting bits and pieces of a novel? Little bits and pieces are for the birds. That's how we feed them. But a healthy Christian needs a full meal deal.

God's word is His-story. If you jumped from place to place in a book about the building of America, you'd be confused about how it was built. God's story is a drama. If you read it from beginning to end you can better see how the drama unfolds. God's word is like poetry. When I'm presenting scripture that I have memorized if I get something out of place or say one word wrong, the rest of it won't come. I have broken the rhythm, the iambic pentameter. It no longer flows smoothly. I know something is wrong. So, I think it doesn't flow so smoothly in bits and pieces either.

People tend to discourage what they will not do themselves. So, there are some who tell me, "How can you possibly get anything out of it reading so fast? I like to take time to think about what I'm reading." That person probably rarely ever reads any part of the Bible. We tend to do all that is possible to keep our excuses intact. People chop down the fasting too. One girl told me, "Oh it's not really fasting. You're taking your meals, just in juice form." But she could never do that. Depriving yourself of anything you normally do, is fasting from it whether it's solid food, pleasures, or TV. On the eighth day of the first fast after AS, her dad, and I did the Omni Theater, I went to a gathering of people from church in an eating-place. But I wasn't eating; I was drinking (that could sound bad). Some noticed and asked about it, at that time the whole church was supposed to be picking days out of the 40 to fast and pray. When I told them that I had been fasting for eight days one guy said, "I had a friend in the service who fasted like that. He did fine for eight days. Then on the 8th day his heart stopped just like that (snapping his fingers). "That was my first time fasting more than one day. I wasn't sure of anything. But I trusted God to guide me. I had to just reject from my mind people's discouragement.

I've read the Bible completely through like a novel nine times now in the short span of 40 days. I have a friend and a Christian brother who has done it in 75 days. I get so much more out of it that way. You know how people say that every time they read a passage or a book in the Bible they get something new out of it? That's very true; do you know why? Because the next time you read a passage or a book of the Bible you are a different person. That is especially true when I read the Bible once a year. By the time I get back to it God has worked on me tremendously, based on the Bible reading and on things happening in my life. I'm not even looking at it through the same eyes. My mind is continually renewed. I'm seeing things in a whole new way.

Here is an example: I didn't know that Saul tried to wipe out the Gibeonites. I didn't notice that before. But when I read it through this 9th time, I got it. God had been teaching me things about keeping covenants over the past year. So, when I read that Saul broke a covenant, my mind is interested. I'm all ears (or eyes) what did he do? If you're curious as to what that's all about, read II Samuel 21.

That's another benefit of reading the whole Bible. You would never know what is being talked about in II Samuel 21 if you haven't first encountered that story in Joshua 3. The Gibeonites acting craftily, came to the Israelites pretending to be travelers from a far country, and got them to make a covenant to let them live. Joshua did that without consulting the Lord, and then later discovered that the Gibeonites were living within the borders of Canaan. They should have been wiped out along with the Amorites, the Hittites, the Parasites, etc. But since Joshua had made the covenant, they had to let them live. They made them slaves instead of killing them. Then when David was king, there was a famine in the land. David sought the Lord to see why. God said it was for the Gibeonites whom Saul put to death.

Here's another one: I didn't know that the sons of Ephraim were cattle thieves. I had been writing my autobiography earlier in the year, and I wrote about a time when I stole something. So, this time I notice that. I Chronicles 7:20-22. It says, *Ezer and Elead were killed by the men of Gath because they came down to take their livestock. And their father, Ephraim, mourned many days.* I'm mentioning this one because I want to also tell you this: The first eight chapters of I Chronicles are genealogies. People don't like to read them because they're not interesting, they don't get anything out of hearing those names that they don't recognize anyway. And there are also many other lists of genealogies. When you read the Bible in bits and pieces there's no way you can get anything out of the genealogies. But when you read it all the way through like a novel, you will love reading through those names because you'll recognize many of them. You'll say, "Oh yes, that's where that guy came from. Or hmmm, land of Uz, that's where Job lived." And I memorized the genealogy of Jesus, so I like to watch the lists close to see which families God chose to have that honor.

Now here's something that tickles me: After being in the Spirit talk class and listening to the discussion about those who still hold to the letter of the law and push the Spirit aside, I read something in Isaiah that I've read many times but didn't understand it like I do now. And for the last nine years God has been opening my mind to what blasphemy of the Holy Spirit is. Isaiah 28:10 says, ***Order on order, order on order, line on line, line on line, a little here a little there.*** That's just exactly how we read the Bible and believe that God is dealing with us, according to every letter of the law. We look for His orders (commandments). We try to make sure we don't leave any line out; we've got to get it all. We read a little here and a little there and think we are getting the whole picture of what God wants us to do. That's what He's talking about here. It was happening way back then. He talks about those who sit in judgment of others. He talks about the way they interpret the message. He talks about how they miss the point: To give rest to the weary, to help each other, to treat everyone with love, to live by the guidance of the Spirit. God Himself, through the prophet Isaiah, is mocking that mentality. It is much easier to understand some of the prophecies if you read the whole Bible like it was meant to be read. It tickles me so much because I missed that before.

I Take mine Straight

It is so wonderful to read the Bible straight through. I see things like: II Chronicles picks up where I Chronicles left off. The end of II Chronicles is the same as the beginning of Ezra. The genealogy in Ezra should be the same as the one in Nehemiah but there are some differences in the numbers, and it makes me wonder, and to know that two men counting will get two different counts. I see that the Chronicles, Ezra, Nehemiah, and Esther are in chronological order. One story follows the other.

I am made to know, after wading through the blood of bulls and goats for days on end, the whole point of the Old Testament. It all leads us to Jesus. It makes us know that we could never make it on our own. It shows us our need for a savior. It is our tutor. It teaches us a lot about the way God's people are to live, not beating commandments into our heads, but showing us the natural expression of love. It shows the way things would all work together effortlessly if we would just love one another.

I'm writing all this while I'm still reading in the Old Testament; but the New Testament shows us even better the loving way to live. It shows us how to live by the Spirit, not by the letter of the law. It shows us that savior that the Old Testament made us know that we needed. It shows us that if we just love God and each other we will be naturally keeping the law with no effort. ***If you love me, you will keep my commandments,*** those who sit in judgment of others keep hollering. Order on order, line on line, while we are missing the deep meaning: If you love me, keeping my commandments will be the natural expression of your life. The commandments are leading us to love, not strife over who's right and who's wrong.

Reading the Bible straight through is not a prerequisite to going to Heaven. It is not a condition of our salvation. Reading the Bible at all is not a condition of our salvation. But after reading it nine times through, and memorizing some of it, I am well able to tell you that it will set you free when it finally sinks in. The New Testament is so liberating. The "Order on order, line on line" mentality says that Jesus made the commandments harder. He added more to them. You have heard that it was said, you shall not murder. But I say to you that whoever is angry with his brother has just as good as murdered him. (I'm paraphrasing). Jesus is not making the commandment harder. He is saying, this is what it says, and this is the deep meaning. And without Me you won't make it. Come to me all ye who are weary and heavy laden, and I will give you rest from that struggle. You don't have to strive so hard anymore. I have kept all the commandments for you. Now all you need is Me. I am the door. There is no other way.

Chapter 16
What would Intimacy with God Look Like?

I was asked the question one time, "What would intimacy with God look like?" And even after I proceeded to tell the man, he didn't get it. He said, "It's impossible to have intimacy with God. No one can have intimacy with God. He's a Spirit; we are flesh. It can't be done. Yet Proverbs 3:32 says God is intimate with the upright. And there are other verses that tell us God wants intimacy with His Children. This is what I said to that man:

When I woke up at 4:00am the first day of the fast of 2003, as soon as I threw one leg over the side and nothing grabbed it, I sprang up; and immediately God brought this great big awareness into my mind. He said, "My Spirit fills the universe!" Wow, I love it when He does that! That was authenticating the fast again. That was telling me that He was right there with me. And in Jeremiah 23:24 it says, ***Do I not fill the heavens and the earth?" declares the Lord.*** God is much bigger than we think. Everything that exists is in God.

So, I said, "If God were and ocean, each one of us would be a drop of water. We are all part of that ocean. If we keep ourselves separate from that ocean we can easily be seen. But if we had intimacy with that ocean, it would be like putting the drop of water back in. Then we would be so in tune with God, so much a part of Him, that we could not be seen at all. We would be lost in Him. We would be so much in the Spirit that the flesh would no longer be visible."

Don't you think that God wants us to be that close to Him? Wherever He waves, we would wave with Him. But He would have some of us waving, while others would be inside the whale's belly. Others would be floating a boat. I would probably be keeping the fish alive inside the minnow bucket. Everyone would have their own responsibilities in the ocean kingdom according to their talents. But we would all be lost in God, intimate with Him, following His every instruction, obeying His voice. The self would not be seen. It wouldn't be so important. It wouldn't be the center of anything.

The more we know about God the closer we can be to having intimacy with Him. The more we understand what He is trying to tell us with the whole Bible, the better we can relate to Him. Then it would be easier to find our own little place in the ocean. We would be in there with so many drops of water that we would all look the same. We would all be a part of each other. We would all comprise the body, the ocean. We wouldn't see different denominations. We would all be working together for a common cause. There wouldn't be one denomination out there pushing a beach ball and telling all the others that is what we are here for.

Chapter 17
The End of my Fasting

I began the eighth fast in 2005 with all the exuberance of any other. But I tried to do it with just water like a friend, RM, had done. I made it for three days. On the evening of the third day, I was in church on that Wednesday night. When we stood up to sing my body grew immediately weak. I was taking on pain in every joint. I sat down but had to slump over a little and close my eyes.

Sometimes I wish it were okay to sleep in church. But no one would understand. You've got to be up and running or people will look at you. I was freezing; the air conditioning was too cold for me. I slept a little then it was the end of the service.

One Sunday morning, years ago, my son was sleeping in church. I nudged him and said, "Wake up Ricky."

He said, "Daddy, I'm not sleeping, I'm praying."

So, maybe they thought I was praying.

I barely dragged myself out of that auditorium. I can't even call it staggering; I was too weak for that. I made it to the bathroom for a pit stop. Then I dragged myself to room 109 to be prayed for. While the Elder was praying, he was also laying hands on me. His warm touch revived me, and I walked out upright without any trouble. Did you know you could transfer body heat by just holding hands or touching each other? My kids and I used to do that during the long winter evenings in our great big house that didn't hold much heat.

Then I knew I had just gotten too cold. I went outside for some wonderful heat. Shortly, I felt like I could drive home. I stopped on the way to pick up some V8 Juice. I had to have something a bit more substantial than water. After leaving the store I immediately opened a V8 and hungrily drank in the welcome nutrition in long draughts.

I had begun driving because I was still five miles from home and I wasn't feeling too good at all. About a mile from home I got nauseated. I stopped on a country road and knelt behind the truck. I began to talk to God. I had already been entreating Him to let me know what was happening and what I should do about it. I didn't want to abandon the fast completely.

Just then the occupant of that property came running out to see what was up. He was afraid I was going to do something on his lawn. I told him that I was just feeling a little sick, and it would pass over in a minute. I said, "A drink of water would help." He ran to his car and came back with a bottle of water. I began to drink thirstily and then spewed it out. It was extremely warm because it had been closed up in the car all day. I thanked him and left. I had to make it home to some nice cold water. I had surely gotten heated up fast after leaving the church.

When I got home, after taking a good cold drink, I laid down in my welcome bed. The pain, which was in every joint, had left when the Elder prayed for me. But in a few hours, it was back. I talked to God and asked Him to let me know very clearly if I should eat something.

At the end of the fast of 2001, I had a craving for Graham Crackers with whipped cream. And the following year it was Pumpkin Pie with whipped cream and coffee. I began eating the Pumpkin Pie regularly after that fast because I discovered it would take away headache pain. And I developed a dependency on Pumpkin Pie and coffee. The Pumpkin Pie had to come from Wal-Mart; and the coffee had to be Clover Valley from the Dollar General. Now let me tell you this: Before I met AS I had never seen the inside of a Dollar Store. And I didn't do much shopping at Wal-Mart. Now they are two of my favorite places. And when I die, I'm going to be buried at Wal-Mart so AS will come visit me regularly.

At midnight that Wednesday night my body was racked with so much pain I couldn't sleep any longer. I had not been able to go more than two days without Pumpkin Pie for the last few years except during the fast. I would get the headaches, but they would leave in a few days and not come back until sometime after the fast. This was different. The pain was unbearable. I talked to God again, then got up and had a piece of Pumpkin Pie and Clover Valley Instant Coffee. I returned to bed and instantly the pain was gone. I slept comfortably; and when I awoke, I was still comfortable. So, I continued with the fast for another 24 hours.

The following night I went to sleep around 9:00 and I woke up at midnight with a body full of pain again. I asked God again if I should go back to eating. I had been easily keeping up with prayer and Bible reading because this is my second year of fasting while I have rest from my labors. I got up and had a piece of Pumpkin Pie and Clover Valley Coffee. Instantly the pain was gone.

The next morning the pain was back again. No matter how much juice I drank, the pain persisted. So, I had something to eat for dinner that day. The pain immediately left. That to me was a clear indication that I should go back to eating. So, I felt comfortable in ending the fast. God had allowed it to go for seven years; and on the eighth year He called it to an end. Seven is the perfect number.

I continued with the Bible reading and Prayer during the eighth year, and now on into the ninth. Miracles continue to happen in my life. I will tell you of a miraculous thing that occurred during this ninth fast. I'm not fasting from food this time. I can't call it a fast from TV, because I haven't watched it in 17 years. So, this year I tell friends that I'm fasting from sin, because my preacher is against it.

Before I tell you about this year's blessings. Let me tell you what happened in 2005, early in the year before the fast. The story begins to ripen in September of 2004 just after the fast. I found my long-lost twin. But listen to what the Lord has done in our lives. First, the search:

Chapter 18
The Ground Search

On September 25th, 2004, I went to Friendship, Wisconsin for my mom's 80th birthday party. Her birthday is on the 15th, but we celebrated it on the 25th. I had put together a family picture with all eleven of us adult sons and daughters, including my twin, who has been gone from the family since about age thirteen, and a brother who died at age twenty-five. My twin and I had been put in different foster homes; she at age thirteen, and I at age sixteen. I kept up with the family in my adult years, but she didn't. So, no one in the family had seen her for thirty-seven years; except that I had searched for her and had found her and visited with her twice, briefly, the last time being at our 20-year high school reunion in 1993. Then I lost track of her again.

Now, Billy Graham came to Fort Worth, Texas in 2002. While our church was preparing for that, I was handed a brochure advertising his mission. Out of fifteen faces on that brochure my twin's picture jumped out at me; and at that moment God laid it on my heart to begin searching for her again. I had tried unsuccessfully to find her by telephone in 1999 while I was vacationing in Minneapolis.

In preparation for my mom's birthday, I scanned her picture from the brochure into my computer along with that of all of us. I had made an exotic wood, contrasting wood frame, with all our birthstones around the inner perimeter. I didn't know at all how to get the pictures into a collage like that;

but while I was fooling around with it on my computer, the pictures jumped into place, already arranged according to age. I had not previously arranged them; they were scattered in the computer. I got them all in one file, but not in order, and somehow shazam, they jumped into place. Do you think God was helping me? Here's a photo of the frame and all of us: My twin is right in the middle and I'm in the middle right.

Now when my family saw her picture amid the rest of us, they were amazed. They didn't believe it was she. I think I would know my twin anywhere; but I had no proof.

Before going into Wisconsin, I spent some time in the Minneapolis area on chance that I might be able to bring her with me to my Mom's birthday party. I first stopped in Lakeville because I had heard her mention that town. I stopped on the main street of that small town and walked into a grocery store.

I had done a search on the Internet before my trip; and it didn't turn up any favorable results at all. It threw a bunch of Jeannie's in front of me of every different age and said, "For $50.00 we'll give you all these addresses." I said, "No way! I don't want those addresses." But in that grocery store my hopes were boosted. I was talking to people and having lots of fun; but nobody knew her. Then a young lady stepped up and said, "Yeah, I know Jeannie and Mark. But they're not together anymore. They divorced eight years ago." She said, "Jeannie remarried and has an eleven-year-old daughter named Kim." And she gave me the new surname, which didn't prove to be right. But most of her other information was perfectly correct. Except for remarrying and having an eleven-year-old child. One of the store employees called that couple's number and then told me, "No, that's not the right one." The way she said it left doubt in my mind. I thought, "Maybe she's still avoiding us even after she's remarried."

I walked across the street to the Ben Franklin 5 and 10 cent store. I immediately encountered a middle-aged woman who works with Mark (that was Jeannie's husband). She took a few of my cards and promised to give him one and ask him to contact me on my cell number. I didn't expect that he would call, and he didn't.

I couldn't learn anything more in Lakeville, so I went looking for a room for the night. I ended up in Hudson, Wisconsin before I found a suitable hotel. Then I asked God, "What am I doing in Hudson, Wisconsin in this expensive hotel? I'm supposed to be looking for Jeannie in the Minneapolis/St. Paul area. I think I lost already." But soon I found out what I was there for.

There at a Denny's Restaurant one of God's prayer warriors was stationed to pray for me; and I prayed for her. We had a couple of hours of lively conversation. I told her many things about my life, and all about my search for Jeannie. And she told me all about what God is doing in her life, about her studies in college, and about massage school. Then we held hands and prayed, hugged, and parted.

In the morning, I got information at the Wisconsin Visitor's Center that led me to 7203 158th St. in Apple Valley. The whole story is wonderful. Miracles happened, one right after another. Apple Valley didn't mean anything to me; I was sure I was to begin in Eagan because that's where I had found her, by a stroke of luck, (God's blessings) in 1986. But I jotted down the address for Mark and Susan Runnels in Apple Valley. I really didn't want to find that guy. He isn't friendly with me. He kept Jeannie away from her family; and he tried to keep me from talking with her at the high school reunion. I had told him, "I think if my sister didn't want to associate with me, she'd let me know." I was sure I wouldn't get any help from him. And I didn't. He didn't call me when that girl gave him my number.

So, I was happening on down the streets that the girls at the Visitor's center had directed me to take to get to Eagan. And suddenly there was a sign that said Apple Valley. I said, "Oh my goodness, Father, there's that town. Now what was that address?" 158th Street, just then the streets began getting close to that number. I had to make a couple of turns, and there it was. I rolled down 158th and the houses started getting close to 7203. I said, "Lord, I can't just drive up to that house. Mark is not friendly with me. I don't even know if this is the right Mark Runnels. And I can't drive around casing the joint. And nobody would be home at this time of the day, and...and...and... it's raining...and suddenly there it was. I rolled to a slow stop in front of the house.

I stepped out of the truck. And lo and behold! A lively-looking girl about my age came skipping out of the house (it had just stopped raining) coming out to her vehicle. She looked at me and said, "Hi! Are you Wes?"

I said, "Yes, and you are Susan?"

We sat down in the garage with the door wide open, a wonderful situation, not uncomfortable for either of us. She proceeded to tell me way more about my twin than I even knew. I cried, and prayed, and shouted, and praised when I heard that my twin has an incredible ability for memorizing Scripture, because that's what I do. I can memorize Scripture at the rate of one chapter per hour. I didn't see Mark, just Susan. She said they think Jeannie lives in Forest Lake. They didn't know for sure; but Mark would love to find her. Could I please let them know what my search turns up? Ooh whoo hoo, Mr. Mark, remember when you had to protect Jeannie from me, and from her family? Now it will be my turn. I thought that but I didn't say it.

I spent three days in Forest Lake talking with people, searching for her, but with no luck. Then I had to head for Wisconsin and Mom's party.

After the birthday party, I went to every place we lived as children and prayed over them for Jeannie and all of us, to be released from the effects of the child abuse that took place there. At some I could only pray over the ground that witnessed the abuse of innocent children because the house was gone. I had already done that in 1992; but I did it again, specifically for Jeannie, after learning some ways the abuse had affected her life. I had gone at God's instruction; and blessings and miracles happened, one right after another.

My most interesting stop was Easton, where we had rented a house from a man named Mr. Grabarski, because every time

I go there, God sends the Sandhill Cranes that are a part of my pleasant childhood memories. During childhood in the woods surrounding that house I explored much of God's creation. But back then I didn't know God. I knew of Him. And I knew He created everything. I still tell Him how wonderful His creation is, that He is a fabulous artist. And I love every little bird and animal.

The Sandhill Cranes are a memory of His wonderful creativity. They landed just as I stopped in front of the house on September 27th, 2004, just as they did in 1992 when I visited there. And just as I had done many times in my childhood, I stalked across the field to get as close to them as I could and take a picture.

I even visited Castle Rock Grade School where I attended 5th, 6th, and 7th grades. The principal showed me around and introduced me to all the teachers. There were no familiar ones; and they didn't know the ones I asked about.

In Marinette I can always find our place at 1908 Lewis Street; but the big house is gone, and the stack of train wheels where I used to hide at age seven and smoke cigarettes is no longer there.

When I first arrived in Amberg, and after looking the whole town over, I stood in front of the only two businesses on the main street marveling at the way the town seemed dead. Just then a woman stopped her truck in front of me, and she and her daughter got out. I told her I was wondering where the Amberg Public School had been. I exclaimed that everything is unrecognizable, and the whole town is like, dead. There are no businesses left and I can't even find the place where the school was like I could have twelve years ago.

She said, "Are you an Allen?" It was Gayle Roush, my cousin. She was able to tell me the name of the road we lived on, Town Corner Lake Rd, and how to get to it. I had figured it out some other way in 1992. Uncle Bud & Aunt Ruth Roush still live on Dow Dam Rd. in the same place they've been all my life. Aunt Ruth showed me around town. Cousin Roy lives on the corner of Dow Dam Rd. and Town Corner Lake Rd. across from where Uncle Ira's place was. Cousin Linda is in Marinette. And there's Connie and a couple others I don't know about yet.

Mrs. Schnabel, my first-grade bus driver's wife, can always tell me more about our family than I know. She said we came to Amberg when my twin and I were two years old and moved out when I was seven. She told me exactly where our house had been located. In 1992 I found the spring where we used to get all our drinking water when I was a child, but this time I couldn't find it.

Was He an Angel

I can't tell you everything that happened along the way; it's just too much. But I've got to tell you about a few of the more amazing blessings. These are the wondrous works of God. As long as we keep telling, He keeps blessing.

Just before driving north toward Green Bay, then Little Suamico, then Peshtigo, then Marinette, then Amberg, and even as far as Iron Mountain, Michigan I just had to stop in Wisconsin Dells. Wisconsin Dells is a famous tourist town. There, people ride the boat ducks, which are big, open-topped greyhound buses that go on land and water. I wanted to see some of the old sights that were familiar in my childhood. Now how could I do all this except that God gave me freedom from the everyday grind at work? And how could I even conduct this search for my twin? Another miracle is coming up about her too.

So, there I was in the exciting town of Wisconsin Dells. I like to look for old classmates who moved out of Adams County where I went to school and migrated to the bigger towns to find work and a life. I parked at a meter, in an angle against the curb, the pavement sloping downhill toward the curb. I stuck enough coins in the meter for a couple hours, and I went to visit Ripley's Believe it or not, after browsing through the chocolate shop. When I came out, I still wanted to explore some more, but I decided to go put more coins in the meter.

Oh, oh! The lights are on. It had been raining and overcast. When I leave the lights on, I can't hear the ding-dong. Sure enough, the battery was dead. I shut the lights off and left it. Maybe after a while the battery will have built up a little charge. I went back exploring some more. When I came back to the truck, it was still dead. I couldn't push it since it was sloping downhill toward the curb. Nobody was around to talk to. Everyone was having fun at tourist attractions. But there was traffic. So, this is what I did. I prayed about it. Then I got out the jumper cables, opened the hood, hooked them to the battery, and stood there holding the other end for someone to pull in beside me and we'd hook them up.

Very simple! No miracle about it. Everyone would know what I want. So, we wouldn't even know if God did it. My Father likes to stand out in a crowd. He likes His works to be seen and known by all. So, this is what happened. Suddenly a young chap about my age comes waltzing along the sidewalk, humming, and fiddling with the knobs on a little red box he carried in his hands. He sees me with the cables, stops and says, "Oh, do you need a boost?"

"Yes, I neglected to turn off the lights and the battery is dead." So, he hooked up his little red box to the battery, the truck started immediately, and I began to put away the cables. Then I looked up to thank him and see if he wanted to be paid. And he was gone. I looked up and down the sidewalk; but I couldn't see him anywhere. You know how people always say, "Do you think it was an Angel?" Well, let me tell you this and you decide. He was smoking a cigarette!!!

No Stopping or Standing

Now, coming back south from Amberg I drove into Manitowoc, Wisconsin to visit my cousin. It was the first day of my third week away from home in Keller, Texas. As soon as I left the freeway and took a few turns I found myself on Wisconsin Avenue. That was nice. That was the street I was looking for. Thank you, Lord, you are always so good to me. I didn't know my cousin's house number, and I certainly wouldn't recognize her car or anything else about her place. So, I pulled over to the side of the street to call my sister and see if she knew the house number.

As soon as I began to dial the number, a traffic officer pulled up behind me with his lights flashing. I wasn't particularly worried because I never break any laws. The worst thing I'd ever done in all my life was 40 miles an hour in a 35 zone. If you believe that you'll believe anything. But I said, "Oh Oh, Lord, I think I need your help." The officer walked up to my window and said, "Why are you parked here?"

I thought, "Ya know I probably do look like a suspicious character with Texas license plates and all. He probably is just going to tell me to move on."

I said, "I stopped to make a call. I'm trying to find out an address."

He took my driver's license and walked back to his vehicle to check me out. Then I chanced to look up, which I should have done long ago. You know how we sometimes get focused on something and don't even notice what's going on around us? I cringed. Right in front of me was a sign that said, "No Stopping or Standing."

I said, "Father, I know I need your help now. I have been foolish and wasn't paying attention. But if I get a ticket, it will ruin my whole vacation. The money is getting very low now. If I must spend anything extra, I'll have to make a beeline for home and give up my mission, to look for my twin sister. Father, I hope I will get your favor. You have blessed me so much already."

The officer walked back up to my window and said, "Today is your lucky day! I'm not going to give you a ticket."

I said, "I sure appreciate that. You are very kind. Thank you! And I need all the luck I can get. The sign is right there in front of me "No Stopping or Standing" and I didn't even look." We laughed about that. And he asked if he could help me with directions. I said, "No, I think I'm on the right street. I just need to call and get the house number. I'll find a better place to stop."

As I drove off my mind flooded over with the sudden realization of the miracle that had really taken place there. That was a traffic lane, not a shoulder. I should never have stopped there. I stopped right in the middle of the street to make a call. The officer couldn't get around me. He had to stop behind me, so why not turn on his flashing lights and give me a ticket. I drove away saying, "Thank you, Father, you are so wonderful. Your care and concern for me never cease. Someone has to look out for me when I do such foolish things. I'm glad you are that someone. You help whether I am right or wrong. Thanks for always being there for me!"

God Wants to Bless You Too

It's not just me. God is impartial. God stands ready to bless all His children, all who will walk in intimacy with Him. Have you ever experienced the miracles of God when they seem to come one right after another? When you walk with God minute by minute, making Him a part of every aspect of your life, He is going to have His part in everything you do. And if you're out there telling everybody about the exciting things that God does in your life, what's going to happen? He will just keep on blessing you more and more because He's found someone who isn't afraid to tell people that God did it!

But if you don't talk about His blessings they are likely to stop. The fountain will run dry because there's no purpose to keep it flowing. Therefore, the secret strategy to receiving blessing after blessing is: **No Stopping or Standing**. Let your life keep moving. Keep walking with God. Let your lips keep putting out the message that God blesses His people. Tell of His wonders.

All through the Psalms David says he will tell of God's wondrous works. If he does anything more often than telling, it's praising God for His blessings. Both are good examples to follow, and good habits to acquire. Here are a few examples: Psalms *2:7 **I will surely tell of the decree of the Lord...9:1 I will tell of thy wonders.22:22 I will tell of thy name to my brethren...40:9,10 I have proclaimed glad tidings of righteousness...I have spoken of thy faithfulness...I have not concealed thy loving-kindness...71:16,17 I will make mention of thy righteousness...I still declare thy wondrous deeds.*** Do you want to be blessed like David was? God called him a man after God's own heart. Keep on declaring the wondrous works He does in your life.

Businessmen spend big money for advertising to let the world know that their product or service exists. God gives great and wonderful blessings to those who let the world know that He exists. And His blessings are unlimited because He owns everything. The Bible says He owns the cattle on a thousand hills. If He gives you just one of those hills, you could start a meatpacking plant.

a thousand cattle on a hill Elk on a hill

He is in control of everything; and He can make anything happen. If you really want to be a part of bringing others to God, just start talking about His blessings in your life. God is the one who draws people to Himself. No man has the power to save souls. *John 6:44* ***No one can come to Me unless the Father who sent Me draws him; and I will raise him up on the last day.***

Jesus Christ exists to love and save the world through His people. When we tell of God's wondrous works to non-believers, their hearts are warmed up to Him. And He can draw them to Himself. When we tell of His wondrous works to other Christians it builds our faith. Romans 1:17 From faith to faith, for the righteous man shall live by faith. God wants Tellers who walk by the rule, **No Stopping or Standing**. Will you be a Teller for God?

A Vacation with a Mission

My vacation covered three weeks from September 20th through October 8th. I went to Wisconsin for my mother's 80th birthday; but decided to stop for a few days in the Twin Cities area to look for my twin sister. I drove across the nation telling people about the blessings of God in my life. Starting in the Fort Worth-Dallas area I drove through Oklahoma, Kansas, Missouri, Iowa, Minnesota, into Wisconsin, then to the upper peninsula of Michigan and spent a night in Iron Mountain, then back down through Wisconsin in the Green Bay area, over to Chicago and stayed a few days in North Aurora, then down through Illinois, tagged Kentucky at the bridge across the Ohio River, then ducked back through Cairo and the lower part of Illinois, down the lower leg of Missouri, into Arkansas, tagged Tennessee at Memphis, across Arkansas, through Little Rock, Hot Springs, then into Texas again at Texarkana, through Dallas-Ft. Worth, and home to Keller.

One miracle happened right after another. So as I journeyed my stories got more mind boggling than ever. I had run out of business cards and people were giving me their addresses and saying, "I fully expect you to send me a card." Here's another amazing thing that happened in the Chicago area:

When I arrived at my older sister's place in Aurora, Illinois. She showed me a newspaper ad that had just come out that week. It was an ad for an appliance company in Arlington Heights, which is near Chicago. In the ad was the exact picture of my twin sister that I had copied from Billy Graham's brochure, except it was black and white.

I went to visit that company. I walked up to an executive sitting at his desk and said, "I would like to talk with Mrs. H, the lady in your ad."

He looked at the ad and said, "I've never seen this woman before. She doesn't work here." And he gave me the name of his advertising agent. I called him, and he gave me the name of the company in Seattle, Washington that supplies pictures for ads.

Several months later when I found my twin, she verified that it is her picture. She gave it to the company in Seattle for advertising purposes. Billy Graham got it from that company. My twin did work for Billy Graham for a few years; but she never gave him that picture. God works in mysterious ways His wonders to perform.

Chapter 19
Breakfast in Oklahoma City

All day, the Tuesday before Christmas of 2004, I was meditating on Romans 1:16-18. ***For I am not ashamed of the Gospel, for it is the power of God for salvation to everyone who believes, to the Jew first and also to the Greek. For in it the righteousness of God is revealed from faith to faith; as it is written: "But the righteousness man shall live by faith." For the wrath of God is revealed from Heaven against all ungodliness and unrighteousness of men, who suppress the truth in unrighteousness,***

I was preparing to do a partial presentation of Romans chapter one; and I was asking God, "What does "from faith to faith mean?" If we say it right, it's obvious. But all I had ever heard was preachers running it all together from faith-to-faith. But after God told me what it means we can just put a comma after the first faith and say it like this: From faith, to faith; from your faith to my faith.

I was still thinking about that when I went to sleep that night. God woke me up at 3:00am and was filling my mind with the meaning of all three verses. He said it all began with the faith of Jesus. It was from His faith to the Apostles' faith, from the Apostles' faith to the preacher's faith, from the preacher's faith to the member's faith, from my faith to your faith and vice versa, the building of faith, so the righteous man can live by faith. And He talked about how the wrath of God is revealed.

And He was giving me some examples; and I was asking questions. It was a real conversation with God. But He spoke to my mind silently.

I said, "What about when I go all across the nation telling my stories?"

He said, "From faith to faith."

"What about the time my dad tried to bust a chair over my head, and I was put in jail."

He said, "The wrath of God is revealed from Heaven against all ungodliness." He explained further that His wrath wasn't against my dad, but against the child abuse. I was sixteen years old and tough. I reached up and stopped the chair. My dad came at me with his fists. I reached out my hands to stop him; and I pushed him back. He fell through the screen door, ripping out the screen, and landed outside. He didn't come back in. He got in his car, drove to a phone, called the police, and I was put in jail for Disorderly Conduct.

In four days, I was taken to court and my parents were there. The Judge looked at my dad and said, "Do you want him to come home now?"

"I suppose, if he can be a good boy now," said my dad.

The Judge looked at me and asked, "Do you want to go home?"

I didn't know what would happen to me. I certainly didn't want to go back to that jail. I was thinking of all my dad's abuse. I hesitated for a long time. The Judge was patient.

Then I said, "No, I don't want to go back home."

The Judge looked at my dad and asked, "If you can't take care of the other ten, how can you take care of this one?" And he put me in custody of the Social Services; and I was taken to a foster home.

When I was 37 years old, I wrote a speech about that situation to use in presenting a dollhouse-size model of Judge Vince Sprinkle's courtroom, which I had built, to a Child Abuse Advisory Committee. It is kept at the DA's Office and used to teach kids what goes on in a courtroom, so it won't be such a frightening experience for them in abuse cases. That was the first time I realized that I wasn't the bad guy in that situation. I was put in jail for my safety; and put in a foster home for my benefit.

Wes Allen used Judge Vince Sprinkle's courtroom as a guide for his project.

Man designs miniature courtroom to help introduce children to

A MODEL OF JUSTICE

But that Wednesday morning before Christmas of 2004, God said to me, "I'm the one who stopped that chair. I put you in that jail for your safety. And I put you in that foster home for your own benefit."

I had never realized that. I cried! It still chokes me up to write it. Then God said, "You're going to have a white Christmas this year."

I said, "Oh boy, I've always wanted to have a white Christmas. I haven't been able to go north at Christmas time since I came to Texas 30 years ago."

He said, "You're going to visit your mother for Christmas."

I said, "Wow! That will be nice for her. But I should take a present for her. What would I get my mother for Christmas? She has everything. And she's like me having no wants and desires."

God said, "You are going to present your twin sister to your mother on Christmas morning."

By that time, it was 4:00am. I sprang out of bed. No time for that one foot first stuff. I packed my travel bag while I was still talking to God. He was telling me everything to take along. He had me pack four changes of clothes. I said, don't you think I should pack a few more clothes?"

He said, "You've got enough, take your winter motorcycle suit."

I said, "Oh boy, am I going to play in the snow?"

He said, "Take your heavy mittens."

When I was all packed, I said, "Do you think I should make more copies of the Christmas card?"

He said, "You've got enough, get going."

I said, "Don't you think I should eat something first?"

He said, "Get going! You will eat breakfast in Oklahoma City at 10:00."

I was all packed and on the road at 5:00am. It took one hour to get everything together because God was telling me everything to take. I had no idea how far it was to Oklahoma City. But after I got on I35 and headed north I encountered mileage signs. I determined that I would arrive in Oklahoma City around 8:30 or 9:00.

I said, "Father, you can't be wrong. What am I going to do when I get there? Am I going to pray until time for breakfast?"

By that time, I was driving through the Arbuckle Mountains of Oklahoma; and suddenly a snowstorm came up. Traffic was slowed to 40 miles an hour. I wasn't getting any traction unless I followed in the tire tracks of a big Mac truck. But they could go faster than me. Whenever I tried to keep up with my big Mac I would break into a skid. I would slide, whey whoa, whey whoa from one side of the freeway to the other. But it was as if the traffic was being held back, 100 feet behind me, 100 feet ahead of me, except for the truck I was following.

Whenever I lost my big Mac because I couldn't keep up, I would wait and get behind another truck. I broke into a skid many times. The traffic stayed 100 feet ahead, 100 feet behind. Then I was following a truck that had whiskbrooms sticking out above its tires. It looked like a big Mac with sideburns.

I kept up for a long time with my big Mac with sideburns. Then suddenly, I broke into a wild skid that spun me all the way around on the freeway; and I was heading for the ditch. I said, "Faatherrrr! If I go off the road, I'll never be in Oklahoma City by 10:00." Just then I stopped. I drove right around and got back on the tracks. Traffic was 100 feet behind, 100 feet ahead.

I arrived in Oklahoma City and had breakfast at McDonalds at 10:00 just as God had said. Then I had faith that all things would happen just like He said, and I would find my twin and take her with me to see my mom. But that wasn't what He meant.

I stopped in Apple Valley and talked with Susan Runnels again. I spent Thursday night and Friday in Forest Lake looking for Jeannie. Then I drove to Wisconsin Rapids, Wisconsin and stayed the night at my mother's. We talked a little and watched a Christmas show on TV. I do watch TV sometimes when I am visiting. I slept on the couch.

I had a beautiful white Christmas. There was six inches of snow already on the ground and it snowed on Christmas morning, beautiful, soft, white snowflakes. After breakfast I had a long conversation with my mother. I brought her up to a full knowledge of several things she didn't know. I told her all about my twin, why she disowned the family, how she struggled to live above the effects of child abuse, how she had no children of her own because she was afraid that she would abuse them, how she had tried to commit suicide in high school, and other things. I learned some of those things from Susan Runnels. That meeting had been necessary in the search for Jeannie.

I told her all about me and why I had to leave home and live in a foster home. She wasn't there and didn't know about my dad and the chair busting experience. She only knew what he told her; and it certainly wasn't the truth. She remembered the spaghetti incident but didn't realize that I was trying to save her. My dad had yelled something across the table at my mother, she yelled back, and he ran around to her and started beating her with his fists.

My little brain, at age ten, said, it's the end of the world now, it doesn't matter what I do; but I've got to save my mother. So, I picked up his plate of spaghetti and threw it at him. It sailed over his head and crashed through a window making a big mess. He stopped beating and yelled, "Who did that?" Nobody answered, twelve silent faces stared at him. He knew who did it; but he was so surprised that someone had rebelled against him that he just went to his room and shut the door. It was shortly after that incident that he broke my back.

I told her a lot of things that Christmas morning that had happened to us kids. She didn't know because she was at work. She worked at the hospital as a nurse's aide while my dad stayed home and read books. He had a bad back, he said.

Well, my assignment was accomplished. I presented my twin sister to my mother on Christmas morning. I presented her story. That is probably God's preparation for a mother and child reunion that will take place at some point in the future, hopefully soon because my mother is eighty-two years old.

Remember when God told me to take along my winter motorcycle suit? There was a purpose for that. On the way up I ran out of gas on the turnpike in Kansas. (My gas gauge doesn't work; I go by the mileage.) It was freezing cold. (An engine burns more gas in the cold.) Wind blows openly across Kansas for the lack of trees. I put on the suit and walked for gas. That's a long and wonderful story with miracles too; but I better not take the space to tell it. I used the suit in other situations too. I stayed in Wisconsin for a few days and arrived home on New Year's Eve.

Chapter 20
I Found My Twin in Cyberspace

Shortly after New Years of 2005 I did another search on the Internet for my twin. This time all information given was favorable. I recognized places where she had lived from the information Susan Runnels (her replacement) had given me. So, I paid $50.00 and got twelve addresses and phone numbers. I tried calling a few of the numbers but only got to speak with people who didn't know her.

I wrote a six-page letter and sent it out to all twelve addresses along with a birthday card, and my contact information. One of the letters connected. But it wasn't one of the twelve. It had to be forwarded. Everything done according to God's timing works out. It was necessary to accomplish the preparatory work first. My twin contacted me by email on March 10th, three days before our 50th birthday.

My first words to my sister were, "I love you with all my heart, inasmuch as I know what love is; and I think I know a little more about what love is now than I did when we were together as children."

Her first words back to me were, "This is truly the best birthday present I could possibly receive. Thank you so much and PRAISE THE LORD!!!!!!!"

Jeannie is in Minneapolis, a little north to Forest Lake. I've been up there to visit her several times now. If ever you lose your twin, where is the best place to look? **Twin Cities!**

Here are some things I learned about her: Jeannie has an incredible ability for memorizing Scripture just like me, and she performs in costume telling Bible stories in Mime. Her mission, with her silent stories, is to reach the ones who won't listen. She can make any story come alive with her animations. It takes me about an hour to memorize a chapter of Scripture; it takes her 5 minutes. She has a photographic memory. She said she tells the story in words too as well as mime.

She has poor health; she has a condition in her body that has all the symptoms I have; but they call it Tendonitis. She has single again syndrome. She was married fifteen years then divorced just like me. She didn't know that I was hearing impaired; but she majored in Sign Language in college. She was a sign language interpreter for Billy Graham.

We've both been doing our ministries for years and we didn't know what each other was doing. God brought that about in the lives of twins separated by the distance of a nation, she in Minneapolis and I in Texas. Put us together and witness the spectacular performance when you can see the story and hear it too! Do you think God can use us to bring about good in His Kingdom? I have to convince her that her mission hasn't ended yet. Because of her hard life, in and after divorce, she has given up some things.

God began planning for us to be reunited twenty-five years ago when I found Jeannie by telephone and learned of her general location. Had I not found her in person in 1986 I would not even know what she looks like, the rest of the family doesn't, and they can't believe I found her. I encountered her again at our 20-year High School Reunion in 1993. That was the last time I saw her. I am not the one who did all this. God has a plan for us! These events took place in my life; but God is the one who is making them happen. Had He not given me early retirement I wouldn't have been able to carry out the search.

I am thrilled to no end to have learned all the good things about my twin (especially the photographic memory) because she's thirty-five minutes older than me. That means whatever she is, I'll be that way in thirty-five minutes.

Chapter 21
My Heart Burns

This is the first remarkable blessing of this fast of 2006.

For the last couple of years I have been plagued with heartburn. Everything I eat causes heartburn. But I love even the curses in my life because they always result in a richer blessing. And it's only right that my heart should burn because it's full of the fires of love and with the Spirit of God. I'm not bragging. I'm just telling you these things, so you'll know what to say when you brag on me.

I got medicine from my doctor that took the heartburn away instantly; but the medicine caused upset stomach and the "back door trots." So, I quit taking it.

Then I discovered that vinegar takes away heartburn, actually, AS told me. So, I put a half-teaspoon of vinegar in eight ounces of water and drink it; and that takes away the heartburn. And when I put a half teaspoon of vinegar in my coffee, it doesn't create heartburn. But still, everything I eat causes it.

Then I discovered that all I have to do is eat lots of pickles. Sweet pickles take away the heartburn, but dill pickles take it away quicker. So, I was eating pickles like they are going out of style until I am becoming an old sour puss.

For the last ten years I have been dedicated to God. And I love being dedicated to God because my life is blessed very richly. I have given to Him all that I am and all that I have. I even gave Him all my time, and He portions it out better than

I can. And there is more than enough time for everything. And as a reward for giving Him my time, God gave me back all the time I used to spend working for a living. And I am retired. What a blessing! What a reward for obedience!

I discovered in Numbers 6:2-3 what God told the sons of Israel to do when they take a special vow to the Lord. And one of those things was to abstain from grape juice and all grape products. And once when I was having bladder trouble, urinary frequency, and I couldn't make it passed a bathroom, God said, "Stop drinking the grape juice."

Immediately, I trashed the bottle I was guzzling, and instantly the bladder settled down. And I didn't have to visit that bathroom every five minutes. So I promised God that I wouldn't drink any grape juice except at the Lord's Supper.

Now, when this fast and Bible reading started, I came upon Numbers 6: 2-3. And what do you think it says? **"He shall drink no vinegar."** "Oh boy, sorry Father, I didn't take notice of that before. I can't guarantee that I will abstain from vinegar forever, because I must get rid of the heartburn. But this is what I will do. I will abstain from vinegar for these 40 days of Bible reading. And if the heartburn overwhelms me, so be it." It had been even more intense for the last few weeks.

So I quit with the pickles. And I quit spiking my coffee. That was in the first week that I stopped. And guess what? There is no heartburn. It just doesn't come. It had been a constant thing so I can tell immediately when it stops. God is holding back the heartburn. Wow! It is so wonderful to be dedicated to Him.

It's after the fast now and I'm still without heartburn.

Chapter 22

A Few More of the Miracles

Buying a House

One of the biggest miracles that occurred during the fast of 1999 was buying a house. I had been living in the Woodstone Apartments for eight years. I always kept my rent paid on time. I was a loyal tenant. I respected all occupants of the complex and did good for people as I found opportunity. But one day, very unexpectedly, I got a message from the management saying that they would not be renewing my contract. "You have to be out by January 31st, and we don't have to give you a reason." "Hmmm, where am I going now, Father? Life is exciting!"

That was a miracle; but I didn't know it at the time. For the next six months I stayed with a retired doctor. I worked around the place to pay for my room. I went to work at my job, building furniture, during the day; and worked diligently in the evenings at maintenance and yard work at the doctor's home. I offered seven hours a week to pay for my room. It was accepted graciously. But soon the doctor felt like more hours than that should be given. I was then evicted because I wouldn't comply.

AS and I began praying for and looking for a home for me to buy. She liked mobile homes. We looked at many of them, and houses too. I went to the new mobile home place. They all wanted to sell me one. Some did a credit check; and told me I could buy anything I wanted. That was surprising because my credit rating was destroyed at the end of my marriage. All the mobile home places wanted me to go ahead and buy a home then look for a place to park it. I laughed at that; and I wouldn't knuckle under to it.

I had BJ, my wonderful real estate agent, looking for some land for me in Keller or the surrounding area. I told her I wanted six acres on which I could park a mobile home; and that would be zoned for the establishment of a multi-family mobile home park. She called one day and said, "I found something in Keller. It' not exactly what you want; but you can look at it." As soon as I drove into the yard, I knew this was my new home.

It is an old mobile home on ¾ of an acre, heavily wooded. Back when I was married, we had a big 3-story house on ¾ of an acre. There was also a barn-type shed that would function as the doghouse in case AS got mad at me (if we were ever together). It was the perfect place for me. Forget about the mobile home park. I had a job.

I called and told her that I wanted it; what do I do next? She began looking for financing for me. AS and I had been praying to find a home, and for a way to buy it, since I had no money. I was staying in an apartment that friends had moved out of after buying their home. I had 30 days to stay there until all their belongings were moved out.

At first, we were going to get an FHA loan. The price was $50,000.00. It would be a 30-year note, 8% interest, payment under $400.00, and about $5000.00 down payment and closing costs. That fell through. No one wanted to finance an old mobile home. BJ looked far and wide for financing. Finally, a company in California agreed to finance it. It would be a 10-year note, 13% interest, payment under $800.00, and around $10,000.00 down payment and closing costs. Now where was the money coming from for the down payment and closing costs? I had moved into a hotel room and was paying nearly $1000.00 a month. I couldn't save anything that quickly.

After AS saw the place, she agreed it was the perfect home for me; and we were praying for God to make a way to buy it. When I was told the exact amount to bring to closing and had been working away at getting it together, money started coming in from everywhere. BJ volunteered to give me her commission, the seller donated $1500.00, I built a hot tub enclosure for a friend for $1700.00, I was working overtime and saving all I could, some of that down payment and closing cost got financed into the loan. I went to the closing with a cashier's check for the full amount. It was $600.00 too much; they had to give me a rebate.

I moved in. My sister came from North Aurora, Illinois and stayed with me for a week and helped me clean and arrange the place and go buy things for the home. I built all kinds of yard equipment for adults to have fun with. I built a fire pit for cooking over a campfire, and three picnic tables. I built a swing set with six swings, three derby cars on which we push each other around, a go-kart, an archery range, three horseshoe pits, and a volleyball court. And I purchased twenty outdoor chairs for our meeting area.

Then I invited the whole singles group over for an overnight campout, and to dedicate the home to God. I determined that no sin would take place in this home to the best of my ability and with God's help. I vowed that it would always be opened and available for the benefit of God's people. And to this day I continue to make improvements to the house and property. A big rock house is being built next door. But my place will look equally intriguing. I will not be ashamed of it, and neither will my neighbors. It is a very peaceful and wonderful place. It is beautiful; and I have country-like living.

In 2003 when I lost my job I had been living here for four years. I was ahead one year in principle payments. I didn't know if I would lose this place or not. I didn't know what would happen. My sister in North Aurora had offered me a home with her. That was my "last resort" option. If I had to bail out at the last minute, I would have a place to go.

A woman emailed me and wanted to buy this home. She offered $57,500.00. I wouldn't sell. She and another family that purchased the property next door were praying with all their might that I wouldn't make it, so I'd have to sell. She kept emailing me to see if I had changed my mind yet. I finally told her not to expect that the house would ever be for sale. If I didn't make it, I would rent the house out. I was walking the streets of uncertainty, not knowing what would happen. I put the situation in God's hands. He had given me the home. I was willing to give it up only at His discretion.

As it turned out, in July of 2004 I paid off the house. I had paid very little interest on it. God didn't need an amortization schedule to see which loan was the best deal. If I had paid the note out in ten years it would only have been $32,000.00 interest, while the 30-year note would have been $120,000.00 interest. Since I had paid a year ahead on principle, less of the monthly payment was going toward interest, and more on principle. So at the time I paid it off, less than five years from the closing, the balance was less than half the original note.

The church helped me with the last five house payments during my ten-month saga of unemployment and disability. I gave 10% of the distribution I took from my 401k to God. It was nearly exactly the amount the church had given me for house payments. God prompted me to give it directly to the Brothers Keeper program. And they are happy with me once again.

Now I own my home lock, stock, and barrel. And God owns me; the home, and everything else lock, stock, and barrel. I'm making improvements to it regularly since I have no payment and no bills except utilities. I consider the home self-insured since I have the $100,000.00 investment. This is what happens when you dedicate to God all that you are and all that you have.

Chapter 23
A Blessing from the President

After the fast of 2002 we had a cookout at my place to celebrate God's blessings and praise Him for answered prayer. I had invited everyone on my prayer list to the cookout. George Bush was on my prayer list; and consequently, I didn't leave him out. Along with his invitation I sent a letter telling him all about the fast, and enumerating all things I had prayed for him, his cabinet members, and the government.

I also told him about memorizing our famous historical documents and the speaking I do to lead people to a deeper love for our country, our heritage, and God who gave us our freedom here. I work to lead people to God through our history, because God is in our history. I told him that I memorized his speech "Awakened to Danger and Called to Defend Freedom." That was his congressional address about the September 11th, 2001, incident. I told him I would make it famous for him if it wasn't already.

And I told him about what I have done with using and teaching memory techniques. I told him how it would revolutionize our educational system if memory techniques were taught in schools and colleges.

Now this is what didn't happen: George Bush didn't show up for the cookout. But this is what happened: I sent the invitation in October. On November 11th I received a call from the White House. I was, of course, at work and they had to leave a message. I don't check my messages because I'm hearing impaired. On the 26th of November AS came over and listened to my messages.

She said, "Hey, did you know you got a call from the White House? It's Lisa Van Slyke, from Tom Delay's office. She wants information from you for a press release because they want to honor you with The National Leadership Award."

I said, "Call her back! Ask her what we should do now!"

So AS called and talked with Lisa. She directed us to go to a website and fill out a form giving information for the press release. I had just got on the Internet on September 13th of 2002. I didn't know much about it yet. I found the website; but I didn't find any form to fill out.

AS doesn't know anything about Internet or computers. Lisa could have given her other instructions that she missed telling me. So, I told her, "Call Lisa back and see what we should do now!"

She said indignantly, "You don't have to do anything. They're just going to give you that award. Just wait patiently."

To this day I'm still waiting. Those kinds of things are not as important to AS as they are to me. I would have been totally honored to receive an award from the President. Six months later, on May 14th of 2003, I received a letter from George Bush thanking me for praying for him. It was a 7 x 9 piece of White House stationery sent in a document-sized envelope with a stiff backer behind it so that it couldn't be folded in the mail. He expected me to frame it, and I did.

THE WHITE HOUSE

WASHINGTON

May 14, 2003

Mr. Wes Allen
1149 Blackwood Drive
Roanoke, Texas 76262-8931

Dear Mr. Allen:

Thank you for your kind words of support and for remembering
me in your prayers.

At this time of great consequence for our Nation, I am honored to lead our
country. We pray for the safety of the men and women who serve around
the world to defend our freedom. We also pray for God's peace in the
affairs of men. And we thank God for our Nation's many blessings. I
appreciate knowing that I can count on your support as my Administration
continues to work on issues that are important to Americans.

Laura joins me in sending our best wishes.

Sincerely,

George W. Bush

The letter arrived on a rainy day. The mail carrier couldn't put it in the mailbox because it couldn't be bent or folded. So he put it on the back step leaning up against the doorframe. When I saw that, I laughed. The back step was soaked. Everything was soaked except a little triangular shape around the envelope 1 ½" all the way around. And the envelope was completely dry.

When I saw where it was from, opened it, and read it, I was overwhelmed with feeling. And I praised and thanked God. The envelope could have easily blown away. It could have easily been soaked and the letter ruined. That was another miracle from God. He had kept the letter dry.

Chapter 24
The Best Blessing

Life is very hard sometimes. When we don't know God, we handle things as best we can. When we are living by our own righteousness, we handle things as best we can. But when we are fully dedicated to God, we experience things as best He can. There is a big difference. When you want to do it on your own God is going to let you do that. He gave everyone the choice of free will. He will not violate your choice. But you have the option of giving yourself totally to Him.

When you walk with Him minute-by-minute you have made Him a part of everything you do. When God is walking with you down life's busy streets and danger threatens, is He going to abandon you to face the danger alone? I don't believe He will and neither do you. The only time we get in big trouble is when we don't take God with us on every journey. We think it is impossible to take Him with us everywhere.

Enoch walked with God for 365 years. During that time, he was raising kids. Genesis 5:21-24

Do you think he pushed all the work onto his wife to take care of a home with children and went out strolling through the moonlight with his Heavenly Father? That would not be the acceptable way to walk with God. I think he took care of all his responsibilities while he made God a part of everything he did.

When God is a part of every aspect of one's life, that doesn't mean that bad things aren't going to happen. That doesn't mean that the going will be entirely smooth with no rough spots, with no sand traps, with no pitfalls, with no quicksand. What it does mean is that the rough stuff is going to be just as enjoyable, as delightful, and as easy to handle as anything else. If God did allow you to get hurt, there would be a purpose for it. And it wouldn't be to teach you a lesson because you did wrong, as some would say. God is not an abusive father.

And God is not holding us to a strict set of commandments and cracking the whip if we start to slip. Anyone who looks at God like that doesn't know Him and doesn't have a very good relationship with their Father. But neither is He tolerating a life of sin without any restraints. One must read the whole Bible to get a clear picture.

There is a purpose for commandments or laws. A criminal is placed on probation and required to go through some counseling to bring about a change in his behavior in lieu of being locked up. The behavioral change doesn't take place instantly when he is arrested. He is given a list of guidelines to follow while he is in rehabilitation. He isn't going to be inclined to stay within those guidelines if nobody is watching to make certain he does. So, they are made mandatory, they are commandments; and a penalty is set for the violation of the rules. And when his counseling is finished, if it has been successful, there is no longer a need for the list of rules. They are written on his heart. He knows how to behave for the safety of all those around him.

By the same token, when a person comes to Jesus and becomes a part of God's family he doesn't immediately know how to behave like a Christian. He needs something to guide him. He is given the indwelling of the Holy Spirit, which is his conscience. And he is also given something to show what his life is to be like. The Spirit turns him away from the wrong and guides him toward the right, which he is learning, from all his studying in the Bible. Without the commandments, rules for right living, how would he know what the Christian life is to look like?

After he becomes a mature Christian (I just noticed that says, amateur, with U on the other side of the E <u>lect</u>) he no longer needs a list of rules to follow. They are written on his heart. God isn't binding us with laws today and punishing us when we break them. Romans 4:8 says: ***Blessed is the man whose sin the Lord will not take into account***. Who is that man?

God is looking for the good in us and reinforcing it so we can grow. He works with the reward system rather than harsh punishment. Did He punish David for his great sin? Did He give David 39 lashes for murder and rape? It wasn't recognized as rape back then, but it is now. A man in authority can't take a woman under his authority and do as he pleases. But God didn't overlook David's sin either. He pointed it out to him and saw that he repented. And He made good come out of it. That relationship put Solomon on the throne. Solomon was Bathsheba's second son. Because of that relationship we have the Wisdom of Solomon. Because of David's sin, good was brought about in the world.

When David recognized his sin, he changed his heart and presented his members to God as instruments of righteousness. He fasted and prayed for their first child who was sick unto death. But the child died because that's what God had determined for him. After the death of his child David didn't mope around wallowing in shame. He had already given the situation to God; then he showed the world a man who could live above the wrong he had done. He did good for the people. He led them in the ways of God. He ruled with righteousness and justice. He remained a good example for us.

Since he had presented his mind and his hands to God as instruments of righteousness he wrote most of the Psalms. He raised Solomon to be God fearing and wise enough to ask for wisdom instead of riches or long life. Then when Solomon made his own mistakes and drifted off into idol worship, he was man enough (just like his father) to recognize his wrongs and repent. And when he returned, he wrote Ecclesiastes.

Now, I told you all that to tell you this: the best blessing in all of scripture is found in Romans 6:12-23. Verse 19 states the blessing: ***For just as you presented your members as slaves to impurity and to lawlessness, resulting in further lawlessness, so now present your members as slaves to righteousness resulting in sanctification***.

To the degree that we present our members to God as instruments of righteousness we are sanctified, set apart, made holy. From what are we set apart? We are set apart from our old sinful ways. We are set apart from whatever we are turning away from. We are set apart from the things that are harmful to us. We are set apart from trouble so that though we walk in it, it can't harm us. A Christian is not set apart from everything all at once as soon as he/she is baptized. It's a process of submitting things to God and presenting those members as instruments of righteousness.

So, if you dedicate to God all that you are, and all that you have, including your time, you are in effect presenting those things to God as instruments of righteousness. What happened when I presented my time to God? I did that in 1998, and I still worked for a living until 2004. Since I gave Him my time, He portioned it out: some for work, some for play, some for Bible reading, some for prayer, some for every little thing so that I was never stressed out for lack of time and having to rush. I always had time for AS; but sometimes she didn't have time for me. I did lots of extra things in addition to my job on which I also worked lots of overtime. But it didn't consume all the time. There was still enough to go around for everything. God set me apart from the rat race. That's one of the best things from which to be set apart. That's the only way to live a stress-free life.

And in the end God set me apart from the working world so I didn't have to go back.

It's not an honorable thing, nothing to be proud of to be retired because of disability. But I am pleased with my life. And I don't let it go to waste. I don't let time go to waste; it's a precious commodity. Time isn't really one of our members. It's the thinking about time that changed. So, it's that part of the mind that was presented to God. My disability doesn't paralyze my life. I have more abilities than disabilities.

Now if you present your money to God. That isn't a member either. Present your thoughts about money to God. Then there will be enough to go around. You will never lack anything. All your needs will be met. So, what is it that God sets you apart from in that case? He sets you apart from your wants and desires. I haven't had to struggle with that in many years. Sometimes I don't have any money; but I don't have any wants and desires either so it's easy to live without it. If it wasn't, I would have been screaming with wants when I went ten months with no income.

I have given God my sinful nature along with the rest of me. He can control it better that I can. If you have a particular troublesome part of your sinful nature, continually present the members that are involved with that to God. For example: I had trouble keeping my eyes in their sockets and my mind on pure and noble things in the presence of beautiful women. So, I present my eyes and my mind to God as instruments of righteousness. It amazed me what happened when I first did that. I lost interest in looking below the shoulders. And when my eyes were presented with the troublesome stimuli they would just immediately find something else to do. It was neat because I had never been free from that before. So, God set me apart from that which had plagued my life. I also lost any desire to go on a cruise, to go to a beach, to go boating, to go to a pool party. Why should I want to go to the source of my troubles? The source is my mind. But it's not good to set the troublesome stimuli in front of the door to my mind (my eyes).

One more thing that will give you so much freedom you will rejoice every day is to present your TV watching eyes to God as instruments of righteousness. I used to watch TV prior to seventeen years ago. I know how distressing it is. I know how harmful it is to the human psyche. I know how it consumes time. I know how it drains the body of life-giving energy by first draining the mind and emotions.

If God picked out the shows for you to watch, how do you think your movie schedule would change? If God did set you apart from TV and movies so you no longer had any desire for them that would instantly free up an enormous amount of time. It would free your mind to be more creative. It would free your heart to soar with the eagles. It would make your life more joyous.

Sanctification is a blessing that money can't buy. It is the thing we are unknowingly striving for with all that we do in life. We want to be set apart from trouble, from poverty, from sickness, from anything that makes life unhappy. It is God's earnest desire to give you something that will make your life better and in which you will be more blessed. He wants to relieve our burdens, not give us a heavier one. He wants to walk in intimacy with each one of us and carry our burdens for us.

Chapter 25
The Bible Reading Contest

You might well know by now that I was conducting a Bible Reading Contest. That may be the reason why you are reading this book. I ended the contest, and I have decided to tell you how long it takes to read the Bible. My first recorded time was 87 hours and 55 minutes. My fastest recorded time was 71 hours and 53 minutes. I have also recorded the time it takes to read each book of the Bible. Not many will read the Bible completely through in 40 days. You could be one of the few. The blessings are tremendous.

After reading this book and learning all that has happened in my life because of Fasting, Prayer, and Bible Reading, I hope you are eager to experience for yourself "knowing God better by reading His books" and seeing what could happen in your life.

Could it even be read completely through and leave the mind intact? One spiritual giant who used to be an elder of the church said, "I wouldn't want to experience what it would do to my mind if I read the whole thing all at once. There's too much in there."

What would happen to the life of the man who would venture to read God's Word from cover to cover like a novel? And if he did it over and over again, would he gain any favor with God? Now you have seen what has happened in my life. And it's delightful! My mind is better than intact; it's transformed. I have now read the Bible completely through 16 times. (I'm writing this statement on 9-19-2009)

"The Word of God is living and active and sharper than any two-edged sword and piercing as far as the division of soul and spirit, of both joints and marrow, and able to judge the thoughts and intentions of the heart." Hebrews 4:12

Once you read the Word of God from beginning to end skipping nothing along the way, your life will be changed forever. You will no longer be the same person.

Now you have seen what it's like to read the Bible from cover to cover. I have read the Bible completely through like a novel in the short span of 40 days; and I have done it nine times now. (sixteen times 9-19-09) You know the remarkable things that have happened in my life as a result of that. I have been blessed beyond all that I could dream or imagine. And you will be blessed beyond your wildest dreams. (2006 is the first year that I recorded the time spent reading, but I've been reading since 1998, now I do that twice a year.)

Now you've read about things that have happened in my life. Now you know how God treats those who honor Him by reading His word, and by dedicating to Him all that you are and all that you have including your time. He is impartial. He will treat you just as well. The exact same things won't happen to you; and you better be glad. Your life is different than mine. What things would God bring to completion in your life? What things would He exalt? What things would He remove? It's exciting to think about!

Do you think I can ever go back to where I was? Can I ever again doubt the existence or the providence of God in my life?

INTIMACY WITH GOD AND MY WELL-WORN BIBLE

You've read my book and have seen what happened in my life. Now read the Bible and see what will happen in your life.

More about Bible Reading

It is so delightful to read the Bible! I hope there will be many more who want to read it through like a novel after hearing my story. There are so many who will not do that. And they will be quick to give you numerous reasons for the stand they take against it. They will do everything they can to discourage anyone else from reading it too because everyone wants to be right. Everyone wants his or her opinion to be honored. And most of all they want to feel like they have a legitimate reason for not reading it.

Christian people blast away at me all the time for reading God's word. Isn't that amazing! Persecution almost always comes from other Christians. God is a rewarder of those who suffer persecution especially when we suffer for doing something He likes us to do. So, I am delighted to receive all the negative feedback anyone gives out. And God has rewarded me greatly. And He will reward you too. I am not anything special.

God understands our feelings even when they are wrong about Him; and He leads us to the right understanding of Him. The first time I read through the Bible I got upset at God about things He did in the Old Testament. I was disgusted to read of all the harsh punishments and deaths that occurred because of sin. That disturbed me because I know that no one is without sin, especially me. I dreaded wading through the blood of bulls and goats. But when I got to the New Testament, I was even more thrilled and delighted than ever to see and to know the extent of what Jesus did for us. Jesus took all that punishment away from us. He bore it all. He perfectly kept the law for us, all the commandments, and then did away with them. He removed sin completely from us and nailed it to the cross. And He bore all the punishment; He endured the wrath of God that we ourselves deserved. And now we are without sin. The powerful blood of Jesus covers them. ***Blessed is the man whose sin the Lord will not take into account***. Romans 4:8

The worst sin that God's people could commit was the sin of idolatry. To put something else before Him who did so much for them enraged Him. And it was so absurd that God's people would turn to an idol made of wood, or stone, or gold and trust in it to be their good luck charm instead of honoring the living God and walking with Him daily. And many people do the same thing today.

Intimacy with God

Chapter 26
Bible Trivia

For just the few hours a day that it takes to read the Bible in 40 days, it is well worth it to understand how God dealt with sin then; and how He looks at us now. It gives one so much more appreciation for the love of God. I usually tell people that it takes an average of two hours a day to read the Bible at the rate of 30 chapters a day. I had never averaged it out. I didn't know that for sure. But now I see that I wasn't very far off. But some sections of the Bible take much longer to read than others.

What part of the Bible do you think takes the longest to read? In other words, in what books of the Bible would you find the longest 30-chapter segments? I thought it would be Old Testament Prophecy. But here's what I discovered: The longest 30-chapter segment of the Old Testament is the 27 chapters of Leviticus along with the first 3 chapters of Numbers. That's where you wade through the deepest blood of bulls and goats, in Leviticus, that's the giving of the law. And the first few chapters of Numbers is the numbering of the people. On their journey to the land of Canaan Israel was 603,550 strong. That was the number of men from 20 years old and upward all who were able to go to war. So, can you imagine that great throng of people marching through the land? When you include women and children it would more than double that number. God said they would be as numerous as the stars of the heavens or the sands of the seashore.

But that wasn't the longest 30-chapter segment of the Bible. What I discovered delights me to no end. The longest 30-chapter segment of the whole Bible is the words of Jesus. The four Gospels took the longest to read. All four Gospels took 9 hours and 15 minutes in total. The longest reading was 3 hours and 30 minutes; and the next to the longest took 3 hours and 25 minutes. That is so fitting! It is altogether perfect!

The shortest 30-chapter reading of the whole Bible is the last 28 chapters of Psalms and the first 2 chapters of Proverbs. That took 25 minutes to read. The middle book of the Bible is Psalms. The exact center of the Bible is Psalms 118:8 *It is better to take refuge in the Lord than to trust in man*. That is so perfect for the center verse of the Bible.

In the Bible we are taught to tithe, give 10% of our earnings to God. If we gave 1% of our time to reading God's word that would be sufficient time to read completely through the Bible. There are 39 books in the Old Testament. 3x9=27 and that is the number of books in the New Testament.

The five smallest things mentioned in the Bible are: a flea, an ant, a tiddle, a gnat, and a mustard seed. To remember that tell yourself this little story and see it happening in your mind: A hyper flea jumped on an ant, who built his hill on a tiddle. The tiddle broke and they fell on a gnat and caused him to swallow a mustard seed.

On what mountain did Noah's ark land? Mount Ararat: To remember that, in your mind's eye, see Noah shooting an **arrow at** it.

On what mountain was Abraham told to sacrifice Isaac? Mount Moriah: To remember that, just see him heaping **more rice** on the fire to keep it going.

On what mountain did Moses die? Mount Nebo: To remember that, just see Moses climbing that mountain. He's an old man, 120 years old. As he climbed the mountain his old **knee** began to **bow**.

What is the first state mentioned in the Bible? Arkansas: It says Noah looked out of the **ark and saw**.

Acts 2:44 says that the 3000 on Pentecost Day were all together in one **Accord**. The question is: How did they get all those people into that little bitty car?

Who was the man mentioned in the Bible who had no parents? Joshua: He was the son of **Nun**.

The Conclusion

Now you have seen some of the amazing things that have happened in my life. We call them miracles; but it is the everyday work of God in a person's life. When we have no human explanation for something good that has happened it's called a miracle. And if it is some unexplained bad thing that happened, we call it a freak accident. With God, both types of occurrences work together to transform a person to the image of Christ.

While God does not usually cause bad things to happen, He makes them work together with the good things. Romans 8:28 ***And we know that God causes all things to work together for good to those who love God, to those who are called according to His purpose.***

I couldn't tell you every miraculous thing that happened. If I did, I'd be writing forever because they continue still as I walk with God minute by minute. God does good things in everyone's lives because He loves His children. But He would necessarily be more active in the life of one who walks with Him every minute of every day. When people ignore God, He is silent toward them also Isaiah 57:11. The Bible is God's message to us. He wrote it for a purpose; and that purpose hasn't ended. He said, "My words will not return to me void." Every time you read God's word it is like they are going out from Him again. Going into your mind they will accomplish much in your life. And when they return to Him, they are refortified with life energy. ***"The Word of God is living and active and sharper than any two-edged sword and piercing*** *as far as the division of soul and spirit, of both joints and marrow, and able to judge the thoughts and intentions of the heart."* Hebrews 4:12 The life is in the blood. The blood is produced in the marrow of the bones. The word of God pierces to the very source of a man's life.

And God said, "My words shall never pass away." Since I put so many of them into memory, where does that leave me?" I memorized The Sermon on the Mount Matthew 5,6, and 7. I memorized the entire book of Romans. I memorized the book of Philippians. And I memorized The Sermon on the Mount in Spanish. I memorized Esther and Ruth. Now I'm memorizing Revelation. I like to think that when we get to Heaven those of us who memorized God's word will get to do the speaking.

And let me mention this: "getting to Heaven" is not my goal. It is not the all-important thing on which I focus. This might help in your intimate walk with God. I have heard many people and preachers of God's word say that their goal is getting to Heaven. If that is the focus, you will do everything that you think it takes to get there. And the destination will be your delight. My goal is for the will of God to be done in my life. I don't focus on Heaven. That is the ultimate fringe benefit. It is a fact that we will be with God at the end of earth-life. I want Him to be able to do with my life whatever He wants. The journey is my delight. That makes even the troubles of life joyous. The will of God is my focus. It will enhance your intimacy with God to keep your eyes on the goal, the will of God not the gift He will give.

There are lots of arguments against reading the Bible like a book. There are plenty of reasons written here in favor of reading it like a book. The choice is ultimately yours. There is always a reward for reading the Bible. The greatest reward is to more completely know God. Children of God should never walk with a stranger. To see what God has done, and why, is to know what He will do. Then you will know Him more completely. Then you will have more delight in the journey. Then you will have richer intimacy with Him.

I'm not saying, with all this, that I have intimacy with God and you don't, or that I have any better intimacy with Him. I'm showing you what I do have in hopes that you can use some of this to enhance your relationship with God. I hope you can use some of it to make your life better and more blessed. I hope you will share it with those who struggle with the problems of life and have trouble finding God or hanging onto Him.

If you choose to read the Bible like a book you will really be the winner of the perfect prize.

9-13-06

About the author

Wesley was born in Chicago, raised in Wisconsin, married in Illinois, spent his working life in Texas, and after retirement, he moved to New Mexico to build hogans for the Navajos. He is a jack of many trades and is highly skilled in woodwork. He has always loved to dream as well as write. In the last several years he has become dedicated to introspection and self-improvement. Over the years he has discovered some important things about receiving healing from above.

Today is April 6, 2024. It has been 18 years since this book was first published. But so much more has happened in the life of the author. Many more miracles and many more blessings have taken place.

He has read the Bible completely through, in 40 days, 53 times now.

He is now living in Thoreau, New Mexico.

He is working on restoring vintage vehicles.

Don't miss out!

Visit the website below and you can sign up to receive emails whenever Wesley J Allen publishes a new book. There's no charge and no obligation.

https://books2read.com/r/B-A-CCTEB-MBABD

BOOKS 2 READ

Connecting independent readers to independent writers.